HYSTERIA 1964

HYSTERIA
1964

THE FEAR CAMPAIGN
AGAINST BARRY GOLDWATER

LIONEL LOKOS

 **ARLINGTON HOUSE**
New Rochelle, New York

Library of Congress Catalog Card Number 67-12382

FOR MY MOTHER AND FATHER

ACKNOWLEDGMENTS

The quotations from *Missiles and Rockets*, found in "Hysteria 1964", appeared on August 17, 1964. Copyright © 1964 by American Aviation Publications, Inc. Reprinted by permission.

The quotations from *Look*, found in "Extremism", are from an article titled, "What Is An Extremist?", which appeared on October 20, 1964. Copyright © 1964 by Cowles Communications, Inc. Reprinted by permission.

The quotations from an article by Seymour Martin Lipset, found in "Extremism", are from an article which appeared in the *New York Times Magazine* on August 30, 1964. Copyright © 1964 by S. M. Lipset. Reprinted by permission.

There are quotations *passim* from articles in the *New York Times*. Copyright © 1963, 1964 by the New York Times Company. Reprinted by permission.

And there are quotations from articles in *National Review*. Copyright © 1964 by National Review, Inc. Reprinted by permission.

CONTENTS

HYSTERIA 1964

HYSTERIA 1964

"The whole campaign against me was run on fear of me."[1]

—Barry Goldwater

Read carefully the history of Presidential politics in this country and you can trace the jagged scar tissue of centuries of political vilification.

You find Tom Paine saying of George Washington: "treacherous in private friendship . . . and a hypocrite in public life, the world will be puzzled to decide whether you are an apostate or an imposter; whether you have abandoned good principles, or whether you ever had any." You find the *New England Courant* warning that if Jefferson is elected, the Constitution would be destroyed. You find some senators comparing Andrew Jackson to Cromwell, Nero, and Julius Caesar, and suggesting that only a Brutus can save the nation from the tyrant. You find the editor of the *Newark Evening Journal* calling Lincoln "a perjured traitor who has betrayed his country, and caused the butchery of hundreds of thousands of the people of the United States."[2]

And yet all of these denunciations combined were almost benign compared with the new high in hysteria reached in the Presidential campaign of 1964. In a period of ten months, Barry Goldwater was accused of:

> being another Adolf Hitler
> fomenting a racial holocaust
> advocating a nuclear policy that would destroy half the world
> seeking to destroy Social Security
> being a lunatic
> wrecking the Republican party
> trying to subvert labor unions
> paving the way for totalitarian government.

Admit that Goldwater threw away the political rule book on the day he accepted the Republican nomination. Admit with *National Review's* William Rusher that "in retrospect, it seems clear that Senator Goldwater made a near-fatal strategic blunder when he confused President Kennedy's fraternal advice against *declaring his candidacy* too soon with the quite different question of when to start *preparing* his campaign."[3] Admit that Goldwater *deliberately* went into the heart of Appalachia and denounced the war on poverty, criticized medicare in Florida retirement country, attacked the TVA in Tennessee and legislative reapportionment in urban areas.[4] Admit all these things, but at the same time admit that the campaign against Goldwater reached a fever pitch of verbal barbarism and demagogic savagery unequalled in anything approaching a civilized society.

Goldwater could not even plan a summer vacation to

the Bavarian Alps without a European correspondent
for CBS concluding that the "American and German
right wings are joining up." Goldwater stormed, "That's
a damned lie," but finally cancelled the trip. However,
he could not cancel what the *New York Herald Tribune's* Evans and Novak called "his image as a militaristic,
bomb-rattling advocate of war, an enemy of peace. The
idea of Goldwater consorting with jack-booted Ger-
mans in Munich embellishes the image," even though, as
the columnists wrote, "it is ludicrous to think of Goldwater in a secret conspiracy with German rightists."[5]

By the middle of September, the Harris Poll reported
that 53% of the women it polled believed that Senator
Goldwater, if elected, would involve the country in war.
Among the men polled, the figure was 45%.[6]

Looking back, after the election, Goldwater commented:

> My opponents built a caricature of Goldwater, and
> this was used by both my Republican primary op-
> ponents and Mr. Johnson in the general election
> campaign. This caricature was built upon a "trigger-
> happy" fellow, "the man who is going to drop the
> bomb," and "the man who would tear up Social
> Security cards." Both of these premises were com-
> pletely false. But this thing started in the primaries
> —and, try as I would, it could not be erased. . . . It
> was entirely a fear campaign.[7]

And there was no scarcity of newspapers ready and
willing to spread the fear from one end of the country to
the other. Throughout the campaign, newspaper support for LBJ had been building at an accelerating clip;

by the middle of October, *Editor and Publisher* reported that 300 dailies endorsed Johnson, while 272 dailies supported Goldwater—*but the pro-Johnson newspapers had three times the circulation of the pro-Goldwater newspapers.*[8]

Early in the campaign, John S. Knight, the highly respected publisher of the *Detroit Free Press,* wrote: "Barry Goldwater is not my candidate, and I have done nothing to promote his Presidential aspirations. But I do think the Arizona Senator is getting shabby treatment from most of the news media." Taking a long, hard look at the syndicated columnists, publisher Knight could find "only a few who are not savagely cutting down Senator Goldwater day after day." As for the editorial cartoonists, they portrayed Goldwater "as belonging to the Neanderthal Age, or as a relic of the 19th century." Knight concluded, "Some editors are disturbed because Barry Goldwater is teeing off on the newspapers and other news media for failing to present the news of his candidacy fairly and objectively. I can't say that I blame him. He hasn't had a fair shake."[9] Since the *Detroit Free Press* later endorsed President Johnson, it is impossible to accuse John Knight of pro-Goldwater bias when he wrote this article.

And in early July, Max Freedman of the *Washington Star* delivered a similar indictment of the European press:

In Britain as in the rest of Europe, there was very little serious attention paid to Senator Goldwater until he won the California primary. Then the gushing springs of prejudice poured forth abundantly. Most of the editors consulted their fears, not their files, and made a talent for invective a wretched substitute for accurate analysis. As a result, Senator Goldwater is being portrayed as a reckless primitive, shooting always from the hip, having a stockpile of prejudices and threats, and incapable of the restraint that sanctifies the exercise of great power. [This caricature] bears no visible resemblance to the truth.[10]

With a lopsided three-to-one circulation advantage in the nation's press, Johnson could count on friendly newspapers to gloss over, or play down, news that could be harmful to his candidacy. And nowhere was this more evident than in the first shooting incident in the Gulf of Tonkin.

At 11:40 p.m. on the night of August 4, 1964, President Johnson told a nationwide TV audience:

As President and commander-in-chief, it is my duty to the American people to report that renewed hostile actions against United States ships on the high seas in the Gulf of Tonkin have today required me to order the military forces of the United States to take action in reply.

The initial attack on the destroyer "Maddox" on August 2 was repeated today by a number of hostile vessels attacking two U.S. destroyers with torpedoes. . . .

Repeated attacks of violence against the armed forces of the United States must be met not only with alert defense but with positive reply.

That reply is being given as I speak to you to-

night. Air action is now in execution against gun-
boats and certain supporting facilities in North
Viet Nam which have been used in these hostile
operations.[11]

Defense Secretary McNamara said he had recom-
mended that the President schedule his announcement
for 11:40 p.m. for the following reasons:

1. By that time, United States Naval aircraft had
   been in the air on their way to the targets approximately one hour.
2. Hanoi, through its radar, had then received indications of the attack.
3. The time remaining before the aircraft arrived
   over their targets would not permit the North
   Vietnamese to move their boats to sea or to alert
   their forces.

McNamara told the press, "As you know, the North
Vietnamese Government did not have time to move
their forces. Our attacking aircraft found the torpedo
boats at their docks. The attack was highly success-
ful."[12]

But one dissenting voice was raised to challenge these
soothing, pablum-ized Pentagon press releases. The trade
journal of the aerospace industry, *Missiles and Rockets*,
took caustic exception to what it called "the calculated
truth" about the incident in the Gulf of Tonkin. The
editor of *Missiles and Rockets* wrote:

The credibility of news issued from the Dept. of
Defense has been opened even wider to question by
the lack of candor during the Viet Nam crisis.

President Johnson during his initial telecast concerning the air strikes against North Viet Nam left the distinct impression that the attacks already were under way. Secretary of Defense McNamara told a press conference at 12:02 a.m. EDT, August 5: "I can tell you that some of that action already has taken place. U.S. naval aircraft from the carriers 'Ticonderoga' and 'Constellation', these carriers operating in the Gulf of Tonkin where our destroyers had undergone two deliberate attacks in international waters, have already conducted air strikes against the North Vietnamese bases from which these PT boats have operated."

QUESTION: Can you tell us if the attack is currently under way?

SECRETARY MCNAMARA: It is currently under way.

There was nothing equivocal about these statements. Yet a Pentagon press summary subsequently showed the attack occurred at 1:15 a.m. EDT, August 5, more than an hour after the Secretary's statement and an hour and a half after the President's telecast.

A lame Pentagon explanation of the discrepancy, issued on Aug. 7, included these points:

By that time (the President's telecast at 11:40 p.m.) U.S. naval aircraft had been in the air on their way to their targets approximately one hour. (This would indicate a flight time of 2 hrs. 35 mins. to hit targets which at the most were within 400 miles of the carriers and probably closer, figures oddly inconsistent with the aircraft employed.)

Hanoi, through its radar, had then (when the President spoke) received indications of the attack. (Not only did this fail to explain how the U.S.

knew what Hanoi learned through its radar, it also
conflicted directly with the statement of task force
commander Rear Adm. Robert B. Moore that he
did not think his planes were viewed by Communist
radar before their mission was announced.)

The time remaining before the aircraft arrived
over their targets was not enough to permit the
North Vietnamese to move their boats to sea or to
alert their forces. (Yet a flight leader told newsmen
aboard the carrier that torpedo boats at one harbor
already were dispersing to sea when the planes appeared. Others reported heavy antiaircraft fire on
the first strikes.)

Unless the Pentagon can clear up these incon-
sistencies—including its failure to explain until
trapped the pre-announcement of the strikes—the
impression must remain of an incredible military
blunder.[13]

Naturally, the *New York Times* never mentioned
this devastating rebuttal to the Administration's "calculated truth". The embarrassing facts *Missiles and Rockets* brought to the surface about the Gulf of Tonkin
incident could have severely damaged President Johnson
politically—and apparently this alone made it unfit to
print!

Consistently, the press could be counted upon to virtually ignore some of Goldwater's most important
speeches—speeches that sought to clarify his position on
the most critical issues of the day. In *The Making of the
President, 1964*, Theodore H. White noted that the
Goldwater speech "scheduled for Keene, New Hampshire, on civil rights violence and the need for law and

order was an excellent speech. But if it is reported any-where in more than a paragraph, I do not know of it."[14]

In similar vein, veteran Washington news correspond-ent Richard Wilson had this to say about a foreign pol-icy address delivered by Goldwater before the Channel City Club in Santa Barbara, California:

> This speech was a masterful exposition of firm poli-cies in foreign affairs and how these policies might be adopted and exploited without war. The phrase "without war" was repeated and emphasized by Senator Goldwater several times. Taking this speech entirely as the authoritative exposition of the Goldwater view, it would have been hard to fault him on the grounds of impulsiveness and super-ficiality. He insists that his convictions in foreign policy are identical with those of Dwight D. Eisen-hower and the late John Foster Dulles.[15]

Try to find this speech—or any reference to it—in the newspapers you read. You will not even find a hint of its existence in the pages of the *New York Times*. On the contrary, almost a week after Goldwater delivered this address James Reston complained that the Presidential primary campaign "lasted for three months without really coming to grips with a single major national issue or producing a single memorable speech."[16] You'll find only scant reference to it in a single paragraph in the *Los Angeles Times*.

You will probably have to do as the author did—write to a newspaper in Santa Barbara, California—in the hope that they wrote a comprehensive article on the Gold-water speech and are willing to send you a copy.

To far too many liberal newspapers, freedom of the press became the freedom to refuse to print—or bury in the back pages—news which would benefit Senator Goldwater. As the distinguished political reporter Ruth Montgomery expressed it:

Goldwater's occasional gaffs have been played up out of all proportion. Attacks against him are headlined, while praise is buried in the last lines. . . . The public has a right to know the good as well as the bad. Slanting the news in an attempt to defeat a candidate for elective office is no prettier than the sham one-party elections held behind the Iron Curtain.[17]

Obviously, Goldwater's wisest course was to bypass the press wherever possible, and take his campaign directly to the people by television. The differences between himself and Johnson, he reasoned, could be brought home to the voters in the same kind of face-to-face confrontation that marked the Kennedy-Nixon campaign four years before.

But the same liberals who had screamed so loudly for the Great Debates of 1960 were now horrified at the audacity of Goldwater in making the same request in 1964. Their refusal came first, and their reasons, if any, came later. And in between the refusals and the reasons, the liberal press—with only rare exceptions—considered the whole indecent subject closed.

The formal *coup de grâce* took place in mid-August, when Administration leaders in the Senate defeated by three votes a bill to suspend the equal-time provisions of the Federal Communications Act. This vote ruled out any chance for televised debates between Goldwater and Johnson,[18] and the Democrats heaved an almost audible sigh of relief.

Dean Burch, then Republican National Chairman, challenged the President to debate Senator Goldwater on *paid* TV time, splitting the costs. In reply, Johnson's journalistic allies referred to Goldwater's statement six months before that "I don't think a President of the United States should debate anybody. He . . . could very well disclose secrets that only he knows." Burch responded that he did not want to do anything to imperil national security, and that he would be glad to accept reasonable ground rules that would keep the debaters out of sensitive areas. As a parting thrust, Burch added that Johnson did not oppose the 1960 bill suspending equal time for the Kennedy-Nixon debates when he was majority leader of the Senate.[19]

The following day, Goldwater offered to pay for *all* of the air time needed for a debate with the President.[20] But apparently the consensus of liberaldom's reactions was a resounding "no". Three weeks later Goldwater was still doggedly trying to back Johnson into a TV studio, with this ringing challenge: "Can my opponent talk? What does my opponent have to say? I challenge my opponent, the interim President Lyndon Baines Johnson, to face the issues. I dare him to face me before the world. I ask of him, debate!"[21]

Of course, the President—with the general acquiescence of an adoring press—never did debate Barry Goldwater. But at least one staunchly pro-Johnson newspaper—the *New York Times*—felt he should have, and expressed its position in no uncertain terms:

Since the purpose of a presidential campaign is to pound out the issues for the understanding and final judgment of the voters, Senator Goldwater's renewed demand for a face-to-face debate with President Johnson has merit. A campaign that is only a popularity contest between rival personal "images" or in which both candidates for different reasons evade the issues, is a meaningless affair.[22]

And so the "meaningless affair" of 1964 went on, like some forced march, to its inevitable conclusion—fought on grounds of maximum advantage to Johnson and maximum disadvantage to Goldwater. It was a war of political attrition, designed to run Goldwater ragged and wear him out—keeping him constantly on the defensive while his foes fired a scatter-shot fusillade of scurrilous abuse from all directions—always confident that their most vicious invective would be reported as news by a breathless liberal press.

Writing in an English journal in July, Murray Kempton had predicted that this surely would be the "vilest" campaign in recent history.[23]

He could not have been more accurate. Just how vile the campaign had become was underscored in October by the Fair Campaign Practices Committee. The Committee declared that a record might be set in the use of political smears in the 1964 election campaign. It cited "the use of guilt by association, fraudulent documentation, cruel and unusual punishment of whipping boys, and evasion of differences." In a special edition of its publication, *Fair Comment*, the Fair Campaign Practices Committee stated, "We recall with some nostalgia earlier elections when we observed that most smears were local in origin and effect. Today the worst of them are *national* in scope and effect. Rarely have the reputations of two opponents for the Presidency been pried by so many citizens into the stereotypes of maniac and thief."[24]

By overwhelming consensus of the liberal press, the "maniac" was Senator Goldwater.

The Committee said of all the vituperation and caricature of the campaign: "Usually they distort and obscure content; this time—at least to date—they largely replace it."[25]

The Goldwater-haters had done their work well, as witness *New York Times* reporter Tom Wicker's statement: "Whatever his actual intentions or capabilities, numbers of voters believe he would take various steps that actually would damage them or their interests."

Wicker pointed out that liberals were afraid Goldwater would pull this country out of the UN. Many voters feared Goldwater would drop The Bomb. The elderly feared he would scrap the Social Security program. Negroes feared he would hand them over to Governor Wallace. And the list of fears—and the fearful—went on and on and on. Wicker summarized, "What is interesting about these specific fears is that in sum they produce a sort of mass fear that Mr. Goldwater would act, in some way, outside the vital center, against the national consensus."[26]

As we will see in "A Diary of Defamation", these fears were nourished, sustained, virtually force-fed for almost three and one-half months—from Republican convention to Election Day—through an almost daily press diet of the most contemptible vilification. By the time the vote was taken, this mass fear had grown to a 50-megaton hysteria that stifled all reason, all fact, all of Goldwater's attempts to inject a dose of truth into the campaign.

The reader will have ample opportunity to assess these judgments for himself in the pages that follow. In the succeeding chapters, the spoken and whispered issues of the campaign—nuclear weapons, civil rights, Social Security, extremism—are discussed one by one in terms of the plain and simple facts. Then a chapter on the California primary, which became a liberal Republican dress rehearsal for the hysteria that followed. And finally, "A Diary of Defamation".

Beyond question, Barry Goldwater—and all that he represents—will be a highly emotional issue in the important Presidential election of 1968. It therefore becomes vitally important to know exactly what Goldwater said, exactly where he stood, exactly what were the buried facts that supported his position. Only then can conservatives hope to refute—effectively and convincingly—the hysteria that was 1964, and the frenzied legacy of one of the most loathsome political campaigns in this country's history.

EXTREMISM

In 1964 the hucksters of hysteria deluded voters with one of the most revolting political shell games of the century. With the fond benediction of their journalistic allies they carved the words "radical right" on the first shell. The second shell they labeled "lunatic fringe". The third shell was "fascism". Then, fervently swearing they had seen Barry Goldwater hiding under all three shells at the same time, they called the whole sleazy medicine show "extremism" and took it on a triumphant road tour of the 50 states.

What is "extremism"? This mild inquiry opened up a Pandora's box of all but unanswerable questions. One might as well attempt to define "due process of law", a phrase Supreme Court justices have been wrangling about for the past 100 years, without finding a conclusive, hard-and-fast definition. Specifically, at what point does an American cross the line of honest dissent—and even bitter controversy—into the no-man's-land of rampant extremism? And who is to draw this line? And who is to doubt that a liberal and a conservative will draw two entirely different lines at two entirely different points on the political spectrum?

What are the characteristics of an extremist? His beliefs? His words? His acts? As *National Review* pointed
out:

> The Democratic Party condemns "extremism" in-
> cluding "extreme tactics" . . . But "extremism",
> presumably referring to a far-out point of view or
> ideology is not at all the same thing as "extreme
> tactics"—i.e. a drastic mode of conduct. The Illi-
> nois Voliva cult that believes the earth to be flat is
> extremist in doctrine, but its tactics are as mild as a
> churchmouse's. Possibly, the idea of racially inte-
> grated schools may not be extremist, but sending in
> paratroops to integrate them is an extremist tactic
> in any man's definition. . . . It seems like you've got
> to pick and choose your extremisms.[1]

Months after the election, Goldwater recalled saying
to Governor Romney, "George, what do you mean?
Let's pin this thing down: what is an 'extremist'? I
never got a satisfactory answer." Goldwater continued:
"Again, I've asked Rockefeller time and again. 'Define
for me an extremist.' I certainly don't care for extremists, but is a man an extremist just because he's concerned about the trend of government or the trend of
Supreme Court decisions?"[2]
Walter Lippmann attempted to grapple with the
word, but succeeded only in grandiloquently adding to
the confusion:

> The essence of the matter is that to be an extremist
> is to encourage and condone the taking of the law
> into unauthorized private hands. . . . the distinction

between private violence and public force is the central principle of a civilized society.[3]

Whatever its other faults, the group most often cited as extremist—the John Birch Society—had never been accused of advocating violence. Presumably with this in mind, Lippmann proceeded to add a few more tentacles to his definition:

It is extremism to say that communism is the enemy of the United States and then to declare that Gen. Eisenhower or the New York Times or the anti-Goldwater columnists are working for the public enemy. No private individual has a private right to brand American citizens as traitors.

Fascism, too, was the enemy of the United States, and as we will see in "A Diary of Defamation", Roy Wilkins of the NAACP, Governors Brown of California and Breathitt of Kentucky, and AFL-CIO President George Meany all compared Goldwater and his supporters to the Nazis—but Lippmann never even hinted this vicious invective was "extremist".

Almost as soon as Goldwater declared his candidacy, his foes in the Republican party began linking the Senator with the John Birch Society, and saying—sometimes directly, sometimes indirectly—that a vote for the Arizonan was a vote for Birchite extremism.

They conceded, of course, that Goldwater was not a member of the John Birch Society, and had not asked for its support. Their reasoning went something like this: a move toward Goldwater was a move to the right

—a move to the right was a move to the far right—a move to the far right was a move toward Birchism.

There they were, the self-proclaimed party moderates, solemnly intoning that two plus two equalled five —and anyone who quarrelled with the arithmetic was himself suspected of the most shameless extremism.

This is the way the story broke, as reported in the February 26, 1964 edition of the *New York Times*. The article noted that Joseph Martin, Jr., Republican Committeeman from California, had resigned his post to support Governor Rockefeller in the Presidential preferential primary. His reason? To keep the Republican party "from becoming a branch of the John Birch Society". Martin asserted it was "absolutely clear" that Senator Goldwater, former Senator William F. Knowland (chairman of Goldwater's California advisory board) and "most of the Republicans" supporting the Arizonan were "not members of the John Birch Society and have no sympathy for the radical right." He conceded that "Senator Goldwater is the favorite candidate of many fine Republicans," but added that Goldwater was "also the only candidate who is vigorously supported by the Birchers and the rightist lunatic fringe." Martin concluded, "Inevitably his victory will also be their victory —their mandate to take over the party structure in its entirety."[4]

Martin's statement was more notable for what it did *not* say than for what it did say. He never named names, nor did he ever attempt to estimate how many members of the John Birch Society lived in California, how many were Republicans, and how many Birchite Republicans were supporting Senator Goldwater in the California primary.

The crucial point that Martin conveniently over-looked was that Goldwater did not support the John Birch Society. A few weeks later, the Senator said he had more violent arguments with the Birch Society founder, Robert Welch, "than anybody in the country". Al-though Goldwater refused to denounce the Society as a whole, he emphasized that he did not agree with the Birchites on most points—for example, their demand for the impeachment of Chief Justice Earl Warren.[5] In March, hoping to still the furor over extremism once and for all, he categorically declared, "I seek the support of no extremist groups—of the left or the right. I seek only the support of California Republicans."[6] Five months later, the Senator was to repeat this identical anti-extrem-ist disclaimer in the course of his now-famous speech at Hershey, Pennsylvania,[7] and the press was to react as if the words had been wrung out of him by General Eisen-hower. (*Life* magazine termed it "a tactical concession to the Republican moderates".)[8]

During this time, one of the few numerical estimates of Birch strength was made by Harvey Schechter, re-gional civil rights director for the Anti-Defamation League. A week before the California primary, Schechter estimated that the Birchers had about 7,000 members in their major stronghold of southern Cali-fornia. In this same speech, he stated that the John Birch Society had been "effectively thwarted" in its political activities in this area.[9]

At the Republican convention in San Francisco, this checkmating of the John Birch Society's political ambi-tions was reiterated by former Senator Knowland, who was chairman of the California delegation. He declared that despite the suspicions of some party liberals, there was not a single Birch Society member in the California delegation. In addition, he said that Senator Goldwater did not have a single county campaign committee led by a Bircher. Summing up, he scoffed at the idea of a Birch or "extremist" takeover.[10]

At the convention, the Scranton-Rockefeller forces had been defeated in their efforts to have the Republican platform specifically denounce the John Birch Society. As always, the debate floundered upon the twin questions, "What is extremism?" and "Where do you draw the line?" And there the matter rested, when Senator Goldwater lit the whole smoldering issue into a blazing bonfire.

What happened at the Republican convention is now history; one can visualize school children, down through the years, repeating those eighteen words about "extremism in defense of liberty", followed by teacher's comments about the heavy political cost of the statement. Even now, from the comfortable and reasonably quiet vantage point of hindsight, it seems virtually impossible to determine why Goldwater made the statement in the first place—what he hoped to gain—why he used, in a seemingly approving sense, the word he had been battling against almost from the start of his campaign.

Where did he get this phrase? Probably from Taylor Caldwell, renowned both as a best-selling novelist and a staunch conservative. This is how Miss Caldwell told it, in a letter to the editor of *America* magazine at the height of the campaign:

A considerable time ago—long before he was even considered as the Republican nominee—I wrote

Barry Goldwater and quoted a saying of Marcus Tulius Cicero's, in connection with Cicero's defense of Rome against the evil and violent patrician, Lucius Sergius Catilina. The quotation is from the Vatican Archives, which I read and translated for use:

> I must remind you, lords, Senators, that extreme patriotism in the defense of freedom is no crime. And let me respectfully remind you that pusillanimity in the pursuit of justice is no virtue in a Roman!

Whether that quotation of Cicero's remained in Barry's mind, I do not know. It is still true today, when America is in exactly the same position as Rome was when Cicero was Consul—an office similar to that of the President of the United States. Barry meant just what Cicero meant, and under the same circumstances, and the "liberals" know it only too well.[11]

What Senator Goldwater meant—or didn't mean—was a subject of heated contention, long after the Republican convention ended. In any event, here is the Senator's exact statement, with its striking similarity to Miss Caldwell's quotation:

> And let our Republicanism so focused and so dedicated not be made fuzzy and futile by unthinking labels. *Extremism in the defense of liberty is no vice. Moderation in the pursuit of justice is no virtue.*[12]

This was undeniably one of the most controversial—and damaging—political statements ever made in this country. One would have to go back 80 years to the Reverend Burchard—and his remark about "rum, Romanism, and rebellion", which cost James G. Blaine the Presidency—to find a parallel in American history.

As could easily have been foreseen, Senator Goldwater and his opponents placed the word "extremist" in two entirely different frames of reference. In the weeks that followed, Goldwater cited the American Revolution and V-E Day as "extremist" actions "in defense of liberty"; his foes countered that the Black Muslims were using this phrase to justify racial riots. In one of the few dispassionate comments on the subject, Arthur Krock, in the *New York Times*, noted this dual usage. Krock wrote, "In praising by usage the word 'extremism,' Senator Goldwater was demolishing the principal argument he and his leaders made for excluding it from the platform. This argument was that the word was misleading semantics, because it could be distorted to mean what any doctrinaire might want it to mean."[13]

At a time when Goldwater should have been pressing a political offensive, he was forced to waste precious time defending himself—explaining his words—becoming more and more bogged down in a discussion that would have been more appropriate to a philosophy class than a Presidential campaign.

A way out of the morass presented itself when former Vice President Nixon requested a clarification of the phrase. In his reply, Goldwater, stressing that "misunderstandings" should not be permitted to impair Republican unity, wrote, "If I were to paraphrase the two sentences in question in the context in which I uttered them I would do it by saying that whole-hearted devotion to liberty is unassailable, and that half-hearted devotion to justice is indefensible."[14]

A few days later, at Hershey, the Senator reiterated what he had said back in March: "I seek the support of no extremist—of the left, or the right." He went on: "I have too much faith in the good sense and stability of my fellow Republicans to be impressed by talk of a so-called 'extremist take-over' of the party. Such a thing cannot happen under Bill Miller and me. We repudiate character assassins, vigilantes, Communists and any group such as the Ku Klux Klan that seeks to impose its views through terror or threat of violence."[15]

Far from just shriveling up, the "extremist" debate escalated into a near-volcanic eruption of molten oratorical lava. Back on January 4, a statement by Gordon D. Hall, "a lecturer on extremist groups", to the effect that one out of every 20 Americans belonged to a left- or right-wing extremist organization, rated only a few paragraphs on page 20 of the *New York Times*.[16] But at the height of the campaign, in the October 20 issue of *Look* magazine, the same Gordon Hall (now elevated to "an authority on extremism") was quoted as authority for the statement that "this nation harbors a total of about seven *million* political, racial, and religious extremists." As breathlessly reported by *Look* Senior Editor George B. Leonard: "Hall bases his estimate on circulation of extremist publications, balanced against a cautious weighing of the extremists' own membership claims." Since extremism had now become equated with wildly exaggerated claims and charges, it was little short of fantastic that Hall would put *any* credence in their claims of paid circulation and actual membership. Possibly in order to backstop Hall, *Look* secured a statement from University of California sociologist Seymour Martin Lipset that "national opinion-poll data tend to bear out a five to seven million estimate."[17]

This was the same Seymour Martin Lipset who had written an article highly skeptical of pollsters almost two months before in the *New York Times*. In this article, Lipset wrote: "Knowing the electorate's *general* position on the principles involved may result in serious errors concerning how they will vote on a *specific real* measure." As an example, Lipset cited heavy support in polls for the general principle of civil rights legislation; but when specific civil rights measures were subjected to referendum in various Northern cities, a large majority of the whites voted against them. Lipset concluded: "So, the pollsters may make considerable public errors, and for all anyone knows, they have made similar mistakes in many of their private surveys."[18]

While Messrs. Hall and Lipset were numbering extremists in the millions, *Look* was conceding that "nobody knows exactly how many people belong to the Minutemen or related groups like the Rangers and the Loyal Order of Mountain Men."[19] And if, at this point, its constant readers were groping for a definition of "extremism", *Look* was ready with this little gem: "Extremism is marked by an inability to accommodate change intelligently and peacefully—with the least possible damage to human and property rights."[20] Included as extremists were the Ku Klux Klan and Minutemen—both of which were clearly capable of physical violence—and the John Birch Society, whose violence was purely verbal.

Look told its readers: "The extremist . . . is the elusive yet powerful force in a new U.S. political climate where the central conflict may not be so much liberal vs. conservative as extremist vs. moderate."[21]

Under this implacable take-it-or-leave-it choice—with the liberal press glibly touting LBJ as moderate-in-chief —who, by the sheer process of elimination, would be considered the champion of the extremists? It required little clairvoyance to divine the answer.

"Extremism" became one of the killer words in the Democrats' vocabulary of invective. It was the blanket epithet that throttled any rational discussion of the basic issues of the campaign. Goldwater was an "extremist" in civil rights—he would go to "extremes" in foreign policy—he was too irresponsibly "extreme" to be entrusted with nuclear weapons—he was so heartless in the extreme that he would end Social Security, and let the elderly starve in the streets. With only a change of synonym now and then, this contemptible nonsense became the rallying cry of all who hated the Senator. It was drummed into the voters' heads with almost day-in, day-out constancy by one powerful speaker after another, one powerful publication after another. And, as we will see in "A Diary of Defamation", it even found its way into the sanctuary of the pulpit!

Actually, the *New York Times* was not visibly impressed with the Democratic party's platform on extremism, which condemned "extremism, whether from the right or left, including the extreme tactics of such organizations as the Communist Party, the Ku Klux Klan, and the John Birch Society."[22] The *Times* editorialized: "It required no vast courage to add the John

Birch Society to the list of extremist organizations, merely an exercise in oneupmanship over Senator Goldwater's repudiation of the Ku Klux Klan."[23] The Democratic platform did not condemn the Minutemen, the arms-bearing group that was the focal point of the aforementioned *Look* article. And *National Review* had every right to inquire, in all moderation:

> Down with the Black Muslims, perhaps? Or doesn't their goal of total destruction of the white race in Armageddon, the karate and small arms training of their storm trooper formation, their random-sample murders, qualify as "extreme tactics"?[24]

Above all, of course, it was the John Birch Society that stood out in the public mind as the extremist *bête noire*. But Goldwater opposed any wholesale condemnation because he felt that not all its members were ipso facto extremist. In this belief, he was far from alone. A spokesman for former President Eisenhower stated, "Without expressing any approbation whatsoever about the John Birch Society, and having expressed specifically his resentment of the despicable and false allegations made by the head of the society, the General, at the same time, has said on occasions that he is quite sure that among its members are many devoted citizens sincerely dedicated to the United States."[25]

Even Senator Kenneth Keating—who refused to support Senator Goldwater—seemed to agree with this view. Asked whether he was repudiating the support of members of the Birch Society, and similar organizations, Keating replied, "I'll be glad to have the vote of any loyal American, *and there are some in the extremist groups.* But I don't expect or want the support of the organizations themselves."[26]

Perhaps one can best summarize the whole swirling controversy by pointing out that extremism, like beauty, is in the eyes of the beholder. As seen through Senator Goldwater's eyes, at the end of the year, "We've just seen a political campaign in which I would say extreme measures were used by my opponent to get elected: the use of falsehoods, the use of threats, the use of power. Now, is he a moderate? Not in my book, he's not."[27]

Not in this book, either.

THE NUCLEAR ISSUE

In 1964, there was no longer any room for doubt that the nuclear *test* ban had mushroomed into a nuclear *talk* ban, and even a nuclear *think* ban as well. Lifting these bans was Barry Goldwater's greatest political sin of the campaign—that he discussed the undiscussable, that he thought the unthinkable, that he attempted to pry open the eyes of the slumbering American public long enough to see that there were viable nuclear alternatives, with as many gradations as the steps of a ladder, between the conventional weapons of World War II and the city-destroying strategic nuclear missiles.

As *National Review*'s James Burnham expressed it:

He is, I think, trying to exorcise the tabu that has been laid on the whole field of nuclear weaponry. . . . It is not only tabu for us to use nuclear weapons; it is tabu to think about using them. Only those few persons who—like Rand Corporation scientists and Cabinet members—possess sufficient mana can even consider the problem of whether to use them; and they, only on condition that they end up with a negative conclusion.[1]

New York Times Washington correspondent Jack Raymond explained that the American nuclear arsenal was divided into two separate categories—strategic and tactical.

Strategic nuclear weapons are directed against the homeland and the war-making capacity of an enemy—his factories, missile sites, population centers, etc. Historically, these weapons are controlled by the President as commander-in-chief. Theodore H. White, in *The Making of the President, 1964*, stressed that "Goldwater never questioned the rightness of this control."[2]

Tactical weapons, on the other hand, are directed against an enemy's military forces on the battlefield and the supplies and operations directly supporting those forces. Tactical operations are usually directed by subordinate officers who are actually engaged in combat.[3]

Early in the year, writing in *The Conservative Papers*, Dr. Edward Teller had bluntly warned the country of the crucial importance of tactical nuclear weapons, in this chilling paragraph:

> If we have not prepared for limited nuclear war, the use of Russian tactical weapons would place [before us] the desperate choice of accepting massive defeat or initiating all-out intercontinental war, by our own action. It is my conclusion that the development of the means of tactical war gives us one of the essential tools by which we can counter enemy action in an appropriate manner without escalation.[4]

It was *tactical* nuclear weapons—and only these—to which Goldwater directed his remarks in the 1964 campaign. A week after Goldwater had announced for the Republican Presidential nomination, he accepted *Life* magazine's challenge to clarify his views on foreign affairs. In this *Life* article—his first foreign policy statement as an avowed candidate—he noted: "I have suggested that the Supreme Commander in Europe be given authority over the tactical nuclear weapons appropriate to NATO's defenses."[5]

The imperatives of national security forbade Goldwater to get down to specifics, but he managed to spell out his proposal in somewhat greater detail in an interview with the West German magazine, *Der Spiegel:*

Q. What nuclear weapons are you talking about now?
A. We are talking about tactical nuclear weapons of a very small nature. There is real need for the Supreme Commander . . . to be able to use judgment on the use of these weapons more expeditiously than he could by telephoning the White House. I would say that, in these cases, the Supreme Commander should be given great leeway in the decision to use them or not to use them.[6]

This interview took place in July, around the time of the Republican convention. The Administration bided its time, confident that it could hang Goldwater with his own words, or its own twisted version of his words.

The issue was decisively joined in late August in a speech Goldwater delivered before the Veterans of Foreign Wars convention in Cleveland. Seeking to dispel the old wives' tale about nuclear all-or-nothingness, the Senator declared:

I have suggested, along with many responsible leaders who have considered the problem, that a way
must be developed to provide NATO with its own
stock of small, tactical nuclear battlefield weapons
—what may truly be called, and ultimately will be
called, conventional weapons. And let me stress
that these small, conventional nuclear weapons are
no more powerful than the firepower you have
faced on the battlefield. They simply come in a
smaller package.[7]

In this context, the use of the ordinarily innocuous
word "conventional" was like waving a red flag at a bull.
This word "conventional" was underlined in the mimeo-
graphed text of his speech and became one of the fighting words of the campaign.

The following day Goldwater defined conventional
nuclear weapons as "any weapon carried by an infantry-
man or a team of infantrymen."[8]

If there had been a "hot line" from the VFW convention to the White House, Administration reaction
could not have been swifter, more savage, or more
meretricious. Using the same forum as Senator Goldwater, Deputy Secretary of Defense Cyrus R. Vance
became the first of many to pollute this vitally meaningful discussion. Vance said that "some have suggested that
tactical nuclear weapons are another matter, that they
should be considered 'conventional weapons', no more
deadly than the weapons of earlier days, to be used
without special safeguards."[9] But, of course, Goldwater
had long before insisted upon the "special safeguard" of
control by only one person in NATO—the Supreme
Commander.

Vance asked the VFW delegates: "How 'conventional' was the 'small' weapon over Hiroshima? The typical tactical nuclear weapon has several times its yield, and the nuclear firepower available to a single infantry division is hundreds of times the destructive force of the bombs which destroyed both Hiroshima and Nagasaki."[10]

The same newspaper article that carried excerpts of Vance's speech noted that Goldwater had told newsmen one of the weapons he had in mind was the Davy Crockett missile, which he said had a force of about 40 tons of TNT. The World War II atomic bombs had a force of 20,000 tons of TNT.[11]

Vance went on: "The largest blockbusters of World War II are like hand grenades compared to these infantry-supported weapons of today. . . . 'Small' and 'conventional' are dangerously misleading and totally inappropriate adjectives when applied to any nuclear weapon."[12]

The day before, Goldwater noted that America was working to develop smaller tactical nuclear weapons, and that he could see the day when mortar-size and possibly rifle-size nuclear weapons could be developed. He pointed out that "such weapons could deliver the same firepower on a battalion position" as present infantry weapons, "but with one weapon" rather than several.[13]

But it remained for the old master of political invective, Lyndon Johnson, to drench the whole nuclear debate in a bloodbath of super-bomb nightmares. In his Labor Day speech, Johnson told a terrified audience: "Modern weapons are not like any other. In the first nuclear exchange, 100 million Americans and more than 100 million Russians would be dead. And, when it was

over, our great cities would be in ashes, and our fields
would be barren, and our industry would be destroyed
and our American dreams would have vanished."[14]

From that day on, the mere mention of the word "nuclear" during the campaign—however qualified—con-
jured up horrifying visions of "great cities in ashes".
City-destroying nuclear bomb or small battlefield nuclear weapon, it was all the same. To far too many
mesmerized Americans, it was madness even to *think* of
anything nuclear—and the Presidential candidate who
dared openly to discuss even the smallest of these weapons with the lowest of yields was the greatest madman of
them all.

In this same speech, Johnson admonished his listeners:

> Make no mistake. There is no such thing as a *con-
> ventional* nuclear weapon. For nineteen peril-filled
> years, no nation has loosed the atom against an-
> other. To do so now is a political decision of the
> highest order, and it would lead us down an uncer-
> tain path of blows and counterblows whose out-
> come none may know. No President of the United
> States of America can divest himself of the respon-
> sibility for such a decision.[15]

It was Goldwater's firm belief that the President had
already delegated authority to certain military field
commanders to use nuclear weapons under emergency
conditions. He believed that such standby arrangements
—pre-authorizing use of nuclear weapons in time of open
war—had long been in effect.[16] And, for once, Goldwater found powerful support for his view.

As far back as October 7, 1958, General Earl E. Partridge, former commander of NORAD (North American Air Defense) had told the *New York Times* that his was the only command authorized to fire a nuclear weapon in combat without the specific approval of the President. As General Partridge outlined the situation, the enemy attack might be so swift that NORAD headquarters would not know of the decision to retaliate with nuclear weapons until well after the retaliation had been ordered. Thus, it might be a division commander with the rank of brigadier or major general who would give the order to fire the first nuclear weapon of World War III. Recalling the Partridge interview during the campaign, the *New York Times* wrote that although communications had improved since 1958 "there has been no indication that the specific delegation of authority to the NORAD commander has been withdrawn."[17]

Even more directly to the point, former Vice President Nixon had this to say from his own personal knowledge:

President Eisenhower recognized that in the event of a Communist attack in Europe, a delay of even a few minutes might result not only in losing the war, but would endanger the lives of 250,000 American fighting men stationed in Europe. He consequently provided that if a Communist attack occurred and the President was unable to issue the order for response with battlefield atomic weapons, because of a communication breakdown, illness or other reasons, that power under certain carefully defined circumstances could be exercised by the NATO commander.[18]

Had President Johnson already delegated emergency authority to the Supreme NATO Commander to use nuclear weapons? The *New York Times* believed he had, and reported to this effect on more than one occasion. To cite two instances:

In the *New York Times*, on September 13, Jack Raymond wrote: "There is, however, a widespread assumption in Washington that in certain types of contingencies, the orders to use nuclear weapons have in fact already been issued in advance. Thus, in circumstances that clearly fit an anticipated situation, the battlefield commanders would need no further instruction."[19]

Even his bitterest foes could hardly cavil at Goldwater's wry comment, "If I can be called trigger-happy for suggesting it, what can you call the President for having already done it?"[20]

Again in the *New York Times*, on September 27, Hanson Baldwin, the newspaper's military editor, noted that: "There are certain exceptions which, under some contingencies, or in the case of a specific command, might empower the commander to use nuclear weapons without a prior specific approval by the President." These contingency plans, he said, would go into effect in case of the death or disability of the President, a sudden massive nuclear attack or a communication blackout.[21]

Baldwin was not at all dismayed by Goldwater's nuclear position. He reviewed Goldwater's belief that the NATO Supreme Commander should have a little more discretionary "leeway" to use small tactical or battlefield nuclear weapons in case of Russian attack. Baldwin noted that there was some American and European political and military support for Goldwater's position, and that the Senator's proposal "is neither very revolutionary nor very new. It has been made to appear far more sensational than it is by Mr. Goldwater's own occasional imprecision, the distortion of his remarks and by the political reactions they have evoked."[22]

In Congress, two members of the Joint Congressional Committee on Atomic Energy—from opposite sides of the aisle—were debating Goldwater's nuclear proposals. The Democrat, Representative Chet Holifield, had virtually exhausted the thesaurus of denunciation in his discussion of the Goldwater position. The Republican, Craig Hosmer, listened, then, with brilliantly wry irony, said this of Holifield:

I believe his handling of this subject was an excellent one, showing magnificent restraint. During the time that he spoke he did not on more than one occasion repeat any of the following words and phrases: "shocking misunderstanding", "shocking naivete", "hundreds of thousands of tons of TNT", "utter madness", "God forbid", "let us pray", "dangerous proposal", "dangerous world", "Sword of Damocles", "accident", "miscalculation", "madness", "fragile thread", "trigger the end of our civilization", "massive nuclear war", "open the floodgates", "power to blast and to poison man and his environment", "hundreds of millions of human beings would perish", "colossal physical and genetic damage", "survival of mankind", "awesome atomic truth", "grim reality", "haunted dreams", "solemn responsibility", "fearful weapons", "haunted by the spectre", "hope and pray", and

"nuclear holocaust". The failure to repeat those
words and phrases more than once, and the restraint shown, I believe is commendable.[23]

Then, hacking relentlessly through the thickets of
rhetoric, Representative Hosmer asked this life-and-
death question:

What if a surprise invasion of Western Europe
should be initiated by the Red army? What alternatives would face the President of the United States?

First, the President could unloose those weapons
that the gentleman from California has described;
escalate to a tremendous nuclear firepower; and
thereby invite the Soviets to take the same kind of
action in return.

The President's second alternative would be one
of restraint—not to use these weapons; resort only
to conventional weapons—in which case obviously
the overwhelming manpower of the Soviet army
would soon have Western Europe at its mercy. He
would, in effect, abandon the allies to whom we
have pledged our aid in the event they are victims
of Red aggression.

The only other alternative that would be left to
the President would be to go back to the doctrine
of the days when we alone possessed the bomb, the
massive retaliation doctrine; turn SAC's bombers
and ICBM's loose on Russia. This, of course, would
call for similar action against us on their part. This
is the horrible spectre of all-out nuclear war our
colleague described with many of the adjectives in
his speech.

If that is the situation today, and the President

has no more alternatives than these, then I ask the gentleman from California, notwithstanding his speech, what is the good of it? What is the difference to him or anybody else whether the world is burned to a crisp by the decision of a field commander, a NATO commander, or a President? The result is the same.[24]

Representative Hosmer then pinpointed the real danger in the Administration's whole nuclear program:

Today not only do we fail to possess the kind of nuclear weapons which safely can be delegated to a NATO commander, we do not even have the kind which can be used safely or sanely by a President himself to meet a very possible threat that could materialize. This is a situation so possible that day after day efforts of one kind or another are being made to forestall the imminent collapse of the NATO alliance.[25]

It bears repeating that Goldwater based his position upon an available stockpile of *small* nuclear weapons; the month before, Goldwater had told newsmen he could see the day when mortar-size and possibly rifle-size nuclear weapons could be developed.

Hosmer found ample grounds in fact and in policy for this scathing indictment of the Democratic Administration:

The Kennedy-Johnson administration had ample notice and had the opportunity to have the kind of nuclear weapons in stockpile today that could be

safely used by either the President or by a delegation of authority to responsible commanders; the
kind of weapons that, unlike the conventional
weapons we are forcing NATO to rely upon
today, would not impose the kind of destructive
havoc that conventional weapons wreaked on Europe in World War II and World War I. We
would possess discreet battlefield weapons which
could be used strictly against enemy troops in the
field, and whose effects would be strictly limited to
the battlefield. And with these you could promise
Western Europe a guaranteed deterrent against Soviet invasion . . .

Four years ago, just about this time of the year,
in the campaign between Richard Nixon and John
F. Kennedy, Mr. Thomas Murray, for six years an
Atomic Energy Commissioner, under appointment
of President Truman, wrote an open public letter
to John F. Kennedy and Richard Nixon advising
them that within the state of nuclear technology
that long ago, were the discreet battlefield weapons
I have described, weapons which could have been
developed, be in our stockpiles today. There are the
kind of weapons that could be used to stem a
Communist invasion without at the same time de-
stroying that which we seek to preserve and without in fact endangering civilization to its very
foundations.

That is the indictment, the failure of the Kennedy-Johnson administration to give our scientists
the go-ahead to produce these discreet battlefield
weapons we so tragically lack. That is the issue in
this campaign. If fault there is, it is up to the
present   administration to explain why it has not

pursued in the past, and does not today pursue, development of the kind of discreet battlefield weapons which I have described.[26]

Representative Hosmer was fully aware of the grave problem of radiation in the present nuclear arsenal; he realized, too, that the radioactive content could be reduced. Even that crown prince of denunciatory adjectives, Representative Holifield, suspended the oratory long enough to concede, "this knowledge of how to lessen radioactivity has been in the hands of weaponeers and in the hands of scientists and within the knowledge of our Committee for many years, going back to the Eisenhower administration."[27]

For that matter, Dr. Edward Teller had written months before, "By underground explosions, we have made, in recent years, considerable progress toward the development of clean nuclear devices."[28]

Well, then, what was the Great Nuclear Debate of 1964 all about? As Republican Representative Hosmer saw it, there was really no debate at all, in any meaningful sense of the word:

The real crux of the current argument is not really whether field commanders should be preauthorized to employ suitable nuclear weapons. Senator Goldwater is right in his feeling that they should. The real crux of this argument is that we do not possess suitable battlefield nuclear weapons so to employ, and President Johnson is right in his feeling that field commanders should not be preauthorized to employ the unsuitable ones now in stockpile.

The pity of the debate raging on this political

battlefront so far is that Johnson has been talking about one thing, Goldwater has been talking about another, and neither has made it clear they are really talking about different things. The further tragedy of the debate so far is that nobody yet has pointed out that it is possible for them to get on common ground. This possibility exists within the present state of the nuclear weapons art. It only awaits the proper direction of the effort of our atomic scientists to go about it.[29]

As a member of the Joint Congressional Committee on Atomic Energy, Hosmer was able to speak with considerable authority when he said:

It is possible within the immediate future to develop and quickly place in stockpile tonnage yield battlefield nuclear weapons with such small radiation effects that no concern need be held over the confinement of these effects to the battlefield. On only a slightly longer time scale, it should be possible for our laboratories to supply field commanders neutron-emitting nuclear weapons whose radiation effects are limited to the immediate firing range and whose explosive yield is so slight that physical destruction to cities and structures would be far less extensive than that from use of conventional weapons. In the not too distant future, beyond these first developments, others are in store which would permit a further discrimination in response, truly affording us the "wider choice than humiliation or all-out nuclear action" for which the late President Kennedy so wisely pleaded.

It is important to note that President Johnson at

no time has ever claimed to have ordered the nuclear laboratories to proceed with the developments
I have outlined. If there is fault to be found, it is in
the failure of this initiative.[30]

Finally, Representative Hosmer brought the whole
issue into the arena of cold-war reality, and asked the
frighteningly unanswerable:

> The weapons which we do not have—what hap-
> pens if the Soviet Union possesses them? They have
> capable nuclear scientists. We have no reason to
> believe they are less capable than ours. They have
> talked about these kinds of weapons. As a matter of
> fact, a recent Soviet book on military strategy even
> discusses in a practical way their use. Of course, we
> have no way to prove or disprove that they do not
> have them. But what, I ask you, will be the situa-
> tion if, in fact, they do have them and we do
> not?[31]

The reader will search in vain for any reply by the
Johnson Administration; it would be equally fruitless to
search for any reference whatever to Hosmer's penetrat-
ing analysis in the pages of the *New York Times*.

For all Johnson's evangelistic anti-nuclear fervor, the
hard facts of life were that NATO's defense was based
upon the use of nuclear weapons. The *New York
Times'* military editor, Hanson Baldwin, wrote: "Most
military men believe . . . that the United States Seventh
Army and Allied Forces in Germany would have to use
battlefield nuclear weapons immediately if the Russians
made a massive assault."[32] And the military man who

was in the best position to know—former NATO
Commander Lauris Norstad—told an audience in Roch-
ester, Minnesota, that "the NATO military forces in Europe themselves depend to a considerable extent on nuclear weapons."[33]

The sum total of it was this: that nuclear weapons, in
and of themselves, are meaningless without clear and definite authority to use them. If the Russians throw a massive assault at Europe, either the NATO Commander
must have the authority to use suitable battlefield nuclear weapons, or communications between the battlefield and the White House—back and forth—must be so
instantaneous, so accurate, so complete, that there can be
no possibility of costly delay, military error, or miscalculation by the President.

Could the President give such iron-clad assurances?
Goldwater seriously doubted it; he feared a possible
communications breakdown in time of war. But Defense
Secretary McNamara boasted of a worldwide United
States communications set-up that could put a commander in touch with the President within two minutes,
under any conceivable circumstance.[34]

On September 9, the *New York Times* reported that
the U.S. Military Command was conducting a global
communications exercise, designated "High Heels III".
McNamara said this exercise would continue throughout
most of the month, and commented, "military commanders and staff, as they do periodically, are testing
worldwide communications systems and reporting procedures, under conditions that would exist during a
major enemy attack on the free-world nations." He
noted that the primary purpose of "High Heels III" was

to insure the responsiveness of all such systems and procedures.[85]

A week and a half later, "High Heels III" was caught flat-footed by the second incident in the Gulf of Tonkin.

The morning after this incident took place, the *New York Times'* lead paragraph could only be described as a masterpiece of vagueness:

> Two United States destroyers fired upon, and presumably hit, what they took to be four or five hostile targets . . . in the Gulf of Tonkin, Government sources reported.[86]

But then, what else could the *Times* report when, six hours after McNamara heard of the incident, this was all *he* could tell the press:

> Preliminary and fragmentary reports have been received of a nighttime incident in international waters in the Gulf of Tonkin. There has been no damage reported by American vessels, and no loss of American personnel. The reports of the incident are being investigated. We have nothing further to say until our investigation has been completed.[37]

The following day, McNamara himself read a statement which included this cryptic paragraph:

> CINPAC (the Pacific Fleet Commander) reports that two United States destroyers on a routine patrol forty-two miles from land in the Gulf of Tonkin were menaced by four unidentified vessels

which, because of their dispositions, courses and
speed, indicated hostile intent. The destroyers, after
changing course to minimize danger to themselves
and after the unidentified vessels continued to close,
fired warning rounds. In spite of these warning
rounds, the unidentified vessels continued to close.
The destroyers then properly opened fire and the
approaching craft disappeared without closing suffi-
ciently to open fire on the destroyers.

Immediately after making his statement, McNamara
left, without answering questions. The *New York
Times* noted that "Mr. NcNamara's report which still
left key questions unanswered, was given . . . more than
twenty-eight hours after the first reports of trouble
reached the capital."[38]

Small wonder that Goldwater jibed, "With the great
communications system which McNamara is always
bragging about, they are waiting for an airmail letter to
find out just what did happen."[39]

Some unnamed officials explained that the darkness
and poor weather at sea had made it extremely difficult
for the destroyers and accompanying aircraft to identify
the vessels during or after the confrontation. (The reporters might have asked when was the last time that
hostile vessels did their menacing in sunny daylight.) A
daylight search by ships and planes, about eight hours
later, yielded no further "persuasive" evidence.[40]

Were these hostile vessels from North Viet Nam or
Red China? The *New York Times* could only shrug its
shoulders and write, "The Administration's statement
acknowledged the lack of evidence by avoiding any reference to their identity."[41]

Two days later, President Johnson finally met the press, only to say that no additional information was ever obtained, and that this left him without proof of the identity of the four hostile vessels sighted by radar. The President lamely added, "I don't think I can go beyond that. It is not because I don't want to, but I don't have any additional information."[42]

A week after the incident, the Defense Department was still so confused that it sent a special Navy team to the Far East to try to reconstruct what actually happened in the Gulf of Tonkin. The detailed reports from the destroyers were said to have differed in some important respects from the original reports. And Defense sources said the reports contained contradictory detail that contributed to the confusion and uncertainty.[43]

Goldwater asked whether a cover-up had been attempted by the Administration, or whether there had been confusion of communications.[44] The *New York Times*' editorial writers promptly snapped back, "Amid the welter of unanswered questions, one of the few certainties is that Senator Goldwater was wrong when he implied the United States military communications system had broken down during the incident."[45]

Actually, one of the few "certainties" about the Tonkin incident was that nothing was certain at all! The communications wizards of the Administration had no idea whether the menacing vessels were North Vietnamese or Red Chinese; no trace of boat debris was found, although on the basis of U.S. radar trackings these vessels were presumed to have been hit. It had reached the point where—quoting the *New York Times*—"some doubt was reported to have arisen in some Pentagon circles whether radar actually had detected hostile craft."[46]

Perhaps there was no breakdown in communications as such, but there *was* a colossal breakdown in military reporting. First, six hours after the "event"—then, 28 hours later—what was communicated to Washington was nothing less than hopeless confusion that left the President almost wholly in the dark as to what had happened and what action he should take. This who-are-they, what-are-they, where-did-they-go report may have had its comic-opera aspects; but in a big war—a hot war—the President would have had not days, but only a few desperate hours to make the monumental decisions upon which this nation's safety would depend. In hot war, any delay for any reason could mean the loss of a crucial battle—perhaps even the loss of the war itself. In the nuclear age, time is the one luxury no nation can afford. Small wonder that David Lawrence wrote that in the event of a land attack in Europe "what the military men fear most is that they may not be able to get a decision from the President of the United States promptly enough to rearrange their troops, and also that the frontline situation may be mistakenly assessed by the President and his advisers, far removed from the battlefield."

Lawrence was convinced that discretionary authority would have to be given to the Supreme Commander of NATO to enable him to act quickly in case of an enemy invasion. He added, *The mere fact that such instructions would be known to have been given could prove to be a deterrent of far-reaching significance.*"[47]

The liberals derived sadistic pleasure in deprecating

Goldwater as a relic of the nineteenth century. But in plain and simple truth it was Goldwater who was resolutely facing the future and all its awesome military challenges, large and small. It was Goldwater who had the far-seeing vision to plead for greater flexibility and realism in choice of nuclear weapons, while the provincial left fearfully submerged its head in a conventional sandpile.

As *National Review's* James Burnham wrote, "His critics—using magic and incantations to neutralize nuclear weapons much as the African witch-doctors use spells to turn bullets to water—are attempting the impossible task of turning the clock back to the pre-nuclear age."[48]

THE SOCIAL SECURITY ISSUE

In 1964, the U.S. Budget Bureau estimated that there were 21 million Social Security beneficiaries in America.[1] Barry Goldwater was to alarm at best, or alienate at worst, many of these beneficiaries and the awesome voting power they represented through his use of that fighting word "voluntary".

Perhaps it should be stated at the outset that there were some Americans who were not avid admirers of the Social Security program; and that of these, a few were vocally moving Heaven, Earth, and Congress to let them out of the program altogether. Foremost among these were the Old Order Amish—the "Plain People"—the last of the rugged individualists who asked only to get off the federal gravy train.

The Amish were not opposed to paying income, property, and other taxes. However, they considered Social Security payments not a tax, but policy premiums in a national insurance program which was denied to them by the tenets of their religion. With the consistency as well as the courage of their convictions, the Amish also refused to accept Social Security payments, and were known to shun those who did. An Amish bishop explained their religious beliefs in these words: "We feel it is the duty of the father to help his children get on their own farms. Then, when we get older, we look for the children to return again and take care of us as we need it. So far as Social Security is concerned, we just don't need that. We do not want it. We do not intend to accept it."[2]

But in all its benevolence, government was going to provide for the Plain People's welfare even if it had to seize their property to do it. In one classic case the Internal Revenue Service seized three Belgian mare workhorses from an Amish farmer and sold the animals at auction to pay for the Social Security taxes he owed.[3]

Over the years, various bills were introduced to exempt the Amish from the Social Security Act, but they never quite made it through the legislative process. One of the strongest supporters of such an exemption was Goldwater, characteristically championing the cause of a minority so small as to be without political influence.

Perhaps Goldwater had the Old Order Amish in mind as well as those libertarian malcontents who wanted to provide for their own retirement in their own way when he told the *New York Times*, "I think Social Security should be made voluntary. This is the only definite position I have on it. If a man wants it, fine. If he doesn't want it, he can provide his own."[4] He repeated this statement in Concord, New Hampshire, on the first day of campaigning in the New Hampshire primary.[5]

Rockefeller lost little time in declaring that a voluntary Social Security scheme would wreck the whole Social Security System. The Governor unfurled this charge like a banner in virtually every primary he entered, including the crucial California primary. At a press conference in Fresno, he kindly assured all and sundry that he was not accusing Goldwater of advocating repeal of the Social Security Act. But he was saying that Goldwater's voluntary plan would bankrupt the system. Rockefeller said that about 55 million people were now paying into the Social Security Fund, but the withdrawal of only "a few million" participants would bankrupt it, or force a "steep" boost in payments required of others, or require transfusions from the Treasury's general fund.[6]

Interestingly enough, the entire Social Security reserve fund amounted to 22 billion dollars, *none of which was in cash!* *U.S. News & World Report* drew out Robert M. Ball, Commissioner of Social Security, in this illuminating interview:

Q. Getting back to the [Social Security] reserve fund: in what form does the fund hold that 22 billion dollars?

A. In U.S. Government bonds.

Q. The Government, in other words, has borrowed the money—

A. Yes, and put up bonds for it.

Q. So the money has been spent, and is not there in the fund at all.

A. It is true, of course, that the Government—as a borrower from the fund, just as it would as a borrower from a bank—has used the cash. The fund, instead of holding cash, holds Govern-

ment bonds, and earns a return on those bonds.
The Government has an obligation to the trust
fund, as it would have to an individual or bank
or corporation it had borrowed from. That obligation is to pay interest and repay the principal. . . . To the same extent that the Government's credit is good, the Social Security fund
is sound.[7]

Naturally, this interview took place *after* the election,
when such embarrassing questions could be answered
without wreaking political vengeance upon the Democratic party at the polls. But even if Rockefeller had
been handed this interview on a silver platter, it is doubt-
ful that he would have been disturbed by it; he still
would have singled out Senator Goldwater as the primary menace to Social Security, and *not* LBJ's borrow-
now-pay-later method of financing the Social Security
program.

Early in the campaign, Goldwater started backing
away from the "voluntary" concept, and in his campaign book, *Where I Stand,* expunged the word from his
political vocabulary. "I favor a sound Social Security
System," he wrote, "and I want to see it strengthened. I
want to see every participant receive all the benefits this
system provides." But Goldwater could not resist adding
that the public interest was hardly served "by those who
label every sincere proposal to correct and perfect the
Social Security System as an attack on its basic principles."[8]

Goldwater had voted to increase Social Security benefits in 1956 and 1958, and again in 1964.[9] Nevertheless,

throughout the campaign, the Senator was depicted as a vile monster who would scuttle the Social Security System and, presumably, cause 21 million elderly citizens to be thrown out into the streets.

One of the more rancid memories of the campaign is that of the Democratic party's TV commercial showing a disembodied pair of hands ripping up a Social Security card. As the card was torn, a TV voice said, "On at least seven occasions, Senator Barry Goldwater said he would change the present Social Security System. But even his running mate, William Miller, admits that Senator Goldwater's voluntary plan would destroy the Social Security System. President Johnson is working to strengthen Social Security."[10] Theodore H. White estimated that this commercial, shown over and over again during the campaign, "probably had greater penetration than any other paid political use of television, except for Richard M. Nixon's Checkers broadcast in 1952."[11]

Time quoted one anonymous expert to the effect that if the Social Security System were to be made voluntary, and if only 15% of 1964's covered workers under 30 elected to drop out, the 1965 loss in contributions would amount to $1.5 billion; by 1968, the loss to the retirement benefit fund would amount to $8.5 billion, and by 1988, the Social Security program would be bankrupt.[12]

Actually, these predictions of long-range doom depended upon just how voluntary was "voluntary". There were two possible definitions of the word.

Under voluntary program #1, an American could refuse to make any provision whatever for his old age.

Under voluntary program #2, an American could

choose between public or private old-age pension plans, but would be required to take one or the other.

John Chamberlain, writing in the *Washington Post*, felt that Goldwater had in mind this latter plan. Chamberlain pointed out:

> The original Goldwater statement on [voluntary] social security followed the publication of a poll taken in Britain which indicated that more than 50 percent of the English voters would like to have the opportunity to contract out of Government welfare schemes. "Contracting out" implies that *welfare must be kept up*, but that a choice would be allowed between the public and private kinds.[13]

Under this system—where the worker had to choose between public or private plans, one or the other—would the logical choice be Social Security? The Commissioner of Social Security thought so, in this reply to *U.S. News & World Report*:

> Q. From the standpoint of the typical worker, is Social Security a good buy? Would it be correct to say that no worker could buy private insurance to provide what Social Security does at a cheaper price than the tax he pays?
> A. Yes, I would say that. And it's primarily because of the employer contribution.[14]

Commissioner Ball had previously commented: "Remember that every dollar paid in by an employee is matched by another dollar paid in by his employer. So the employer's contribution is used toward the cost of benefits to those who do not themselves pay the full cost of their own benefits."[15]

If Social Security was so obviously the better buy, why the deathly fear of a voluntary program of "contracting out" that would allow workers to choose between public or private plans? And what basis in fact was there for the loudly trumpeted claim that a voluntary program would bankrupt the Social Security System? As John Chamberlain calmly maintained:

Now it is not true that the American Government is powerless to find a way to finance a social security system that would permit a person to select a public or a private old-age insurance policy, *the qualifying stipulation being that he must maintain either one or the other*. But a presidential candidate would have to take a battery of insurance actuaries along with him to be convincing on this point. And very few people would hang around long enough to listen.[16]

THE CIVIL RIGHTS ISSUE

"For some years, Goldwater has contributed $3 a year to the Urban League in Phoenix, Ariz., but this year he upped the contribution to $50. Goldwater's contributions to the NAACP began shortly after he announced for the Senate on Oct. 1, 1951, when he gave $400 for a special legal fee fund to test segregation laws in Phoenix. . . . In 1955, Goldwater paid a $10 membership fee to join the Tucson chapter of the NAACP."[1]

—Drew Pearson

This was the man who was to be denounced as an ally of Southern racists in the seething emotional cauldron that culminated in the Civil Rights Act of 1964.

We have it on the word of the Rev. Martin Luther King that in January 1963 "high government officials here in Washington were telling me that we did not need civil rights legislation. Even President Kennedy was saying that."[2]

What changed President Kennedy's mind?

Birmingham.

Mention "Birmingham" today and nine out of ten Americans conjure up visions of fire hoses and police dogs used against peaceful Negro demonstrators. This is true enough, as far as it goes. But it is only a minuscule part of the history that was made in Birmingham. In fairness to all concerned, let us attempt to drain the emotion out of the Birmingham story, and see—factually and dispassionately—what actually happened, and why, and whether with a little patience and understanding it all could have been avoided.

Let us go back a month *before* the police dogs were used—to April 2, 1963, when the citizens of Birmingham went to the polls to choose between two candidates for the office of Mayor: "Bull" Connor, the rabidly racist Safety Commissioner, who had been a fixture in Birmingham's government for 25 years, and the more moderate Albert Boutwell, former Lieutenant Governor of Alabama. The votes were counted, and Boutwell won the mayoral election by more than 8,000 votes out of 50,000 cast.[3]

In a profile of the newly elected Mayor, the *New York Times* wrote, "Mr. Boutwell is not an integrationist under any definition of the term. But he is considered a moderate on racial issues, and has always been willing to compromise."[4]

Boutwell was to take over as Mayor on April 15, but the old "lame-duck" city government, including "Bull" Connor, declared its intention of staying in office until October 1, 1965.[5] The issue was taken to a lower court, which ruled in favor of Mayor-elect Boutwell. The Connor group appealed the decision to the State Supreme Court, which set a hearing for May 16.[6]

In an April editorial, the *New York Times* expressed the view that the election of Boutwell offered hope for "a more enlightened approach to race relations", but stressed, "we do not expect that there will be overnight rejection of all the policies that caused so much distress to the Negro community. The Rev. Dr. Martin Luther King Jr. and other leaders of the drive to break down racial barriers ought not to expect it either."[7]

But King and the other Negro leaders *did* expect it. On April 30, Negro integrationists applied to both of the contending Birmingham factions for a permit to stage peaceful protest marches. Both groups denied the request. Mayor-elect Boutwell said the application had been denied by his group because its approval might invite public disorder.[8]

Martin Luther King knew that at this particular time neither group had the authority to redress the Negroes' grievances, even if it wanted to. The Connor group was adamantly segregationist, but still clinging to office pending the results of the State Supreme Court hearing scheduled for May 16. And it was a matter of very public knowledge that until that date—until the court decision that would confirm Mayor Boutwell in office—he was powerless to enter upon any legally binding negotiations with King or anyone else.

With the final court decision less than two weeks away, Dr. King and his group took to the streets of Birmingham, knowing that "Bull" Connor was still Safety Commissioner, still in charge of the Police Department and the Fire Department. The ferocity of Connor's reaction, though not necessarily the form it took, must certainly have been foreseen by King. What happened in Birmingham in those early days of May is

now history. Perhaps the high school textbooks are recalling it already: the 900 students sent out from the
Negro section (700 of them were arrested); the fire hoses
and police dogs used to disperse Negro students protesting racial segregation.[9] But few textbooks will tell of the
aftermath in its entirety—of the Negro riot that broke
out five days later, as at least 2,500 Negroes rampaged
through the business district until they were driven back
by fire hoses[10]—of Martin Luther King apparently no
longer in control of this second, more violent demonstration[11]—of Mayor-elect Boutwell calling for an end to
the demonstrations, promising that "immediate and determined attention" would be given to the city's racial
difficulties as soon as his administration was confirmed
by the court.[12]

Contrary to general belief, not all Southern news-
papers championed Connor and his white supremacists.
To give one example, the *Arkansas Gazette* of Little
Rock stressed that:

> Birmingham voters had just rejected the racist
> "Bull" Connor in his bid for the Mayor's office and
> had elected a new government which is moderate,
> at least by Alabama standards . . . The demon-
> strations immediately following must have sug-
> gested to Birmingham's white moderates that
> Negro leaders were not interested in attaining their
> goals amicably.[13]

Even Attorney General Robert F. Kennedy questioned the timing of the demonstrations. He said he
hoped "for the sake of everyone" that a solution could
be worked out in meetings between both sides and "not

in the streets".[14] What Kennedy did not know was that *before the demonstrations took place* moderate white leaders in Birmingham had attempted to reach a settlement with King, and he had rebuffed them out of hand.

Here is the story, which was consigned to the near-oblivion of page 82 in the *New York Times:*

> The chairman of the Alabama Advisory Committee to the Federal Civil Rights Commission charged yesterday that the Rev. Dr. Martin Luther King Jr. had agreed to secret negotiations with Birmingham business and professional leaders and then had done an about-face.
>
> The Rev. Albert S. Foley, a sociology professor at Spring Hill College . . . said he had pleaded with Dr. King who "at first agreed" and then changed his mind without notice.[15]

Why had King changed his mind?

In the author's opinion, because Birmingham was never really the end King had in mind. This strife-torn city was only a means to the end of a sweeping civil rights bill—far broader than anything previously supported by President Kennedy—blanketing the 50 states. To push the Administration into endorsing such legislation, King needed a racial crisis that would send shock waves across the country and mobilize strong white support for Negro demands. With Boutwell's reputation as a moderate, the whole issue would have become blurred and indecisive. But with "Bull" Connor still in office, King could confidently expect a racial confrontation of crisis proportions.

The national chairman of the March on Washington,
A. Philip Randolph, bluntly remarked to a Socialist
party meeting that "legislation is enacted under pressure."[16] The Birmingham incidents supplied that pressure and put the civil rights bill into the legislative
hopper.

Before Birmingham, President Kennedy had asked
Congress to enact three pieces of civil rights legislation
relating to voting rights, the Civil Rights Commission,
and school desegregation.[17]

A month after Birmingham, President Kennedy sent a
special message to the Congress on Civil Rights and Job
Opportunities, in which he proposed:

> that the Congress stay in session this year until it
> has enacted—preferably as a single omnibus bill—
> the most responsible, reasonable and urgently
> needed solutions to this problem, solutions which
> should be acceptable to all fair-minded men. This
> bill would be known as the "Civil Rights Act of
> 1963", and would include—in addition to the
> aforementioned provisions on voting rights and the
> Civil Rights Commission—additional titles on pub-
> lic accommodations, employment, federally assisted
> programs, a Community Relations Service, and
> education.[18]

That this Civil Rights Act was inspired by fear of
violence was made manifest in the first two paragraphs
of Kennedy's message:

> Last week I addressed to the American people an
> appeal to conscience—a request for their coopera-

tion in meeting the growing moral crisis in American race relations. I warned of "a rising tide of discontent that threatens the public safety" in many parts of the country. I emphasized that "the events in Birmingham and elsewhere have so increased the cries for equality that no city or state or legislative body can prudently choose to ignore them." "It is a time to act," I said, "in the Congress, in State and local legislative bodies and, above all, in all of our daily lives."

In the days that have followed, the predictions of increased violence have been tragically borne out. The "fires of frustration and discord" have burned hotter than ever.[19]

Arthur Krock wrote in the *New York Times:* "the fact is that the Administration is highly apprehensive of racial violence throughout the nation." Attorney General Robert Kennedy was quoted by one senator as painting "a terrible picture of a situation which could become uncontrollable" in an attempt to secure Southern support for the civil rights bill.[20]

In the midst of this long hot summer the Negro groups made plans for a march on Washington to underscore their support for the pending civil rights legislation. The opposition to this massive demonstration was by no means confined to Southerners or conservatives. One of the most outspoken statements on the subject came from Agnes E. Meyer, who had been named to a fifteen-member National Advisory Committee on Equal Opportunity in Apprenticeship and Training. Mrs. Meyer was convinced that "of all the plans for demonstrations now contemplated, none would be more disastrous than the march of thousands of Negroes upon Washington in August to urge the passage of the Administration's civil rights bill. Democratic government itself is imperiled when any group seeks to intimidate the members of Congress."[21]

On August 28, more than 200,000 Americans, black and white, participated in the March on Washington. Their target was Congress. Their goal was passage of the new, more sweeping civil rights bill proposed by Kennedy two months before, and a Federal Fair Employment Practices Act barring discrimination in all employment.[22] The *New York Times* referred to the marchers as a "gentle army", but John Lewis, head of the Student Non-Violent Coordinating Committee, was anything but gentle in the original text of his speech to the marchers. With the verbal violence that sometimes seemed the sine qua non of the non-violent movement, Lewis declared:

> We will not wait for the President, the Justice Department, nor the Congress, but we will take matters into our own hands and create a source of power, outside of any national structure, that could and would assure us a victory. . . . We will march through the South, through the heart of Dixie, the way Sherman did.[23]

And A. Philip Randolph called for a continuation of demonstrations. "You can't move Senators and Congressmen just because a measure is right," he said. "There has to be pressure."[24]

It has now become part of the folklore of the civil rights struggle: the pressure that was applied all across the country in the months that followed. In Brooklyn, fourteen Negroes and whites manacled themselves together and sat down to block the roadway at the Downstate Medical Center Project, which was being built by non-Negro union help. The police had to send for wire cutters and cut the demonstrators apart before they could be packed off in patrol wagons.[25] In Chicago, thirteen members of CORE were arrested at a sit-in demonstration in the lobby of the Board of Education building. They were protesting against the retention of Dr. Benjamin Willis as Superintendent of Schools.[26] The momentum of the civil rights demonstrations was interrupted only briefly by the death of President Kennedy. Less than a month later, more than 2,500 Negroes marched in Atlanta, in sub-freezing weather, to protest that city's failure to desegregate schools, public accommodations, hospitals, and housing.[27] In Nashville, Tennessee—which was considered by white and Negro leaders to have made more progress than most Southern cities in desegregating public and private facilities—police had to use billy clubs to break up a riotous crowd of Negro high school students.[28] And even as far west as Seattle, the pastor of the First African Methodist Church proudly told of "harassment" tactics involving sit-ins and telephone tie-ups at real estate offices that had been active in the campaign against a local housing ordinance.[29]

Almost unheard amid the deafening din of demonstrations was Supreme Court Justice Harlan's deep conviction that the racial controversy was "a clash of competing constitutional claims of a high order: liberty and equality". Justice Harlan firmly articulated the principle

that "freedom of the individual to choose his associates
... and use his property as he sees fit," even though "irrational and even unjust" was "entitled to a large measure
of protection from governmental interference."[30]

Thousands—perhaps millions—of Americans found
themselves virtually besieged by the competing claims of
liberty and equality, by the adamant "now" of the integrationist, countered by the equally adamant "never" of
the segregationist. Among those caught in this withering
crossfire was Senator Barry Goldwater.

During the campaign, a *New York Times* editorial
recalled that "Senator Goldwater's early fervor for extending civil rights by law was so great that he joined
John F. Kennedy and nine other Senators in 1953 in
sponsoring an unsuccessful NAACP bill to prohibit racial discrimination by employers or unions."[31]

In the years that followed, Goldwater lost none of his
interest in civil rights. He voted for the Civil Rights Acts
of 1957 and 1960 primarily because they were directed
at ending discrimination by *government* against citizens.
In 1963, he had offered four amendments to the Youth
Employment Act, forbidding discrimination on account
of race, color, creed, or national origin.[32] But like Justice Harlan, Senator Goldwater felt that laws should not
infringe upon the right of free association among citizens. Goldwater believed that more could be done for
the cause of civil rights at the local level than could be
accomplished by federal fiat, and here the example of the
city of Birmingham lent great practical support to his
thesis.

Earlier in this chapter, we left a Birmingham that was
racked by racial convulsion. Let us now briefly retrace

our steps, and—again draining the emotion out of the subject—see what happened in that city after "Bull" Connor left office.

On May 23, 1963, only three weeks after Connor unleashed the police dogs, the State Supreme Court of Alabama unanimously upheld Mayor Boutwell's right to office.[33] In July, more than 200 leaders of Birmingham's churches, professions, business, and industry formed a biracial committee on community affairs. Mayor Boutwell had appointed this committee on authorization of the City Council. Lauding the event as "an historic occasion", the Mayor said, "this can well be the beginning of our finest hours."[34] In December, Mayor Boutwell stated that the City Council had struck down all city ordinances demanding separation of the races, and had desegregated city buildings.[35]

One of the original demands of the civil rights groups was for city hiring of more Negro employees, most specifically including policemen. The *New York Times* noted that "Birmingham negroes have been petitioning the city for years to hire negro policemen."[36] Arthur D. Shores, a local Negro lawyer, said he was convinced that the city wanted to integrate the police department, but added that officials had never issued a clear-cut statement of policy that would encourage Negroes to apply. In response, the executive assistant to Mayor Boutwell declared that the city had been unable to find a qualified applicant who would take a job on the police force. At least two Negro applicants had turned down jobs on the force, prompting the Mayor's assistant to comment, "we have concluded that they prefer the issue to the job."[37] (By way of a postscript to the Birmingham story: in

March, 1966, Mayor Boutwell was still looking for qualified Negroes to join the police force, and inviting Negro
leaders to help recruit qualified personnel.)[38]

Except for the last event noted, all of these improvements in the city's racial relations took place *before* the
Civil Rights Act of 1964 became law. Perhaps progress
was slow—but progress was made!

As one who had voted for civil rights acts in previous
years, Goldwater refused to close his eyes to the deliberate and studied lawlessness now being wielded as a political bludgeon by civil rights groups. He was disturbed
by the extent of their civil disobedience campaign, and
their arrogant defense of law-breaking when such
law-breaking suited their purpose. And there was cause
to be disturbed when the Director of the Legal Defense
and Educational Fund of the NAACP quoted with approval Martin Luther King's statement that two types of
American laws should be disobeyed: "segregation laws"
and laws that "deny citizens the First Amendment privilege of peaceful assembly and peaceful protest." King
called these laws "unjust".[39] But since there was
scarcely any law that was not considered unjust by
someone, he seemed to be advocating—and practicing—
a kind of selective anarchy. And so it was construed by
such zealots as Lester McKinnie, head of the Nashville
chapter of the Student Non-Violent Coordinating
Committee. "Don't let the jail stop you," McKinnie told
about 200 youths. *"We've got a right to use civil disobedience."*[40] And while society indulgently winked at
King and CORE and SNCC violating laws they disliked,
it grimly ordered total *white* compliance with *all* civil
rights legislation—or else!

In March 1964, Dr. King told some 10,000 civil rights marchers in Kentucky that Negroes must continue to press for equal rights at the risk of being called immoderate. In clear, blunt language, he said that "if moderation means slowing up in our fight, then moderation is a tragic vice which members of our race must condemn."[41]

(It goes without saying that if any right-winger had spoken this disparagingly of "moderation", he would have been blasted as an extremist.)

In the field of employment, Martin Luther King and some supporters wanted, not equal rights, but superior rights for Negroes, in the form of preferential hiring. In the long hot summer of 1963, King declared that "discrimination in reverse" was a good idea.[42] And Jack Greenberg, a high-ranking official of the NAACP, told a *New York Times* interviewer, "where a white man and a Negro are equally qualified, given the need to compensate for past discrimination, the Negro ought to get the job."[43] Some of the most gung-ho white liberals tried to, but could not quite swallow this reverse discrimination. One of the foremost white participants in the March on Washington, the Rev. Eugene Carson Blake, warned that preferential hiring of Negroes was "one of the most dangerous things that any of the Negro action groups have called for." Blake said that if a white man found he could not get a job because he was white, "then you will really have violence."[44] At a press conference in August, 1963, President Kennedy expressed his opposition to preferential hiring.[45] And even Governor Rockefeller felt compelled to caution, "we can't abandon our concepts of equal opportunity for all by giving special privilege to some."[46]

The whole issue was conveniently muted in the debate on the Civil Rights Act of 1964. But perhaps there was still some lingering uncertainty about whether Martin Luther King had really abandoned his enthusiasm for "discrimination in reverse". Or possibly the liberals feared a backlash by infuriated white workers at the polls. But this much we do know: of the eleven sections of the Civil Rights Act, ten went into effect with President Johnson's signature. Only one section—the one prohibiting discrimination in employment—was to go into effect a year later,[47] long after the Presidential election of 1964 had come and gone.*

In the volcanic emotions of the times, anyone who dared question, however logically, the root premises upon which the Civil Rights Act was based ran a grave

---

* The Administration's Machiavellian date-juggling may have been prophetic. In 1966, with Goldwater no longer holding public office, some unions—and at least one racial group—have already begun to feel the sting of reverse discrimination. Following the signing of an "equal opportunity" agreement between the federal government and the Newport News Shipbuilding & Dry Dock Company, a union of company employees filed a "document of protest" with the Equal Employment Opportunity Commission. The union complained that instead of evening things up between Negroes and whites, the agreement actually creates "discrimination by giving some employes rights that others do not have." In New York City, white construction workers are accusing contractors of changing their hiring practices to give more jobs to Negroes, even if they have to lay off some white workers to do it. And in March, 1966, 50 Mexican-American delegates walked out in protest from an Equal Employment Opportunity Commission conference, charging that the commission was indifferent to Mexican-American needs, *and guilty of discrimination in its own hiring practices!* The whole story can be found in the "Labor Week" feature of the May 16, 1966 issue of *U.S. News & World Report.*

risk of being denounced as a racist. And even then, these audacious few could consider themselves fortunate if their writings received more than microscopic mention in the nation's press.

One of the very rare exceptions to the rule occurred when Arthur Krock devoted an entire column to "a profound study of the constitutionality of legislation limiting freedom of choice in personal occupations", written by Dr. Alfred Avins and published in the 1964 winter issue of the *Cornell Law Quarterly*.[48] A Professor of Jurisprudence at Cambridge University, Dr. Avins concluded that the ban of the Thirteenth Amendment against "involuntary servitude" guarantees to "every person *the right to refrain from working for any other person*," and that this guarantee covers "barbers, hotel clerks, shoe-shine men, sales clerks, waiters and waitresses, just as much as . . . fieldhands, cotton-pickers and farm laborers."[49]

Dr. Avins wrote that "in 1964, Negroes are demanding laws to compel whites to serve them in the very same occupations which they themselves were freed from serving whites in 1863, and demanding this under the name of freedom." Avins stressed that "the 13th Amendment makes no distinction as to who enforces . . . labor," and quoted an earlier Supreme Court decision that "the plain intention [of the Thirteenth Amendment] was . . . to make labor free, by prohibiting that control by which the personal service of one man is disposed of or coerced for another's benefit which is the essence of involuntary servitude."[50]

Krock conceded that "not many of those involved are likely to read Dr. Avins' detached analysis of the consti-

tutional issue." But he underscored the salient point that
"Dr. Avins has impressively done as much as can be done
in print to project into the debate on the equal rights bill
a great constitutional issue it poses, and one which has
been carefully avoided or strangely neglected."[51]

The Civil Rights Act of 1964 was debated on the floor
of the Senate for 736 hours and ten minutes, over a period of 83 days. But in spite of all the words—which
filled 2,890 pages of the *Congressional Record*[52]—it was
a debate in which the Southerners were talking almost
entirely to themselves. All the traditional symbols and
trappings of legislative discussion were there, but for all
that, it became abundantly clear that most senators really
didn't give a tinker's damn what the opposition had to
say. Once the Johnson-Dirksen civil rights coalition was
formed, it was all over but the speeches. And the vote on
cloture soon put an end to those.

The Senate coalition was listening much more atten-
tively to the strident voices coming from the ranks of
the civil rights leaders warning that civil disobedience
could give way to criminal violence if the Civil Rights
Act were not passed. Whitney M. Young, Jr., executive
director of the National Urban League, said that if responsible Negro leaders "don't have some victory pretty
soon," they would not be able to control the "Negro
revolution."[53] And the Johnson Administration held an
even more apprehensive view. As the *New York Times*
told it, less than two weeks before Senate passage of the
civil rights bill:

President Johnson is reported to be concerned
about the possibility of violence this summer as civil

rights protests spread throughout the country. . . .
The Administration assumes that the civil rights bill
will be passed more or less in its present form. But
officials are worried that it will not go far enough
to meet the pent-up frustrations of some Negroes—
especially in the North.[54]

Senator Goldwater was well aware of this pressure to
beat the clock and the calendar before another long hot
summer could explode on the streets of every major city
in the country. But even so, he still hoped it would be
possible for him to support the civil rights bill of 1964.

Goldwater's ultimate opposition to the Civil Rights
Act was confined to just two of its eleven sections—the
public accommodations and fair employment clauses,
both of which he considered unconstitutional. In early
June, he told reporters he wanted to support the bill, if it
were softened enough. He added that since he had voted
for previous civil rights legislation, "it wouldn't be out
of character."[55] A week later, he indicated that he could
vote for a substitute bill prepared by Senator Dirksen,
coupled with three amendments favored by Senator
Hickenlooper.[56] A week before the final vote was
taken, Goldwater was still saying that he hoped to be
able to vote for the civil rights bill, explaining that it all
depended upon the bill being modified to meet his objections.[57]

Then the amendments were brought up and, one by
one, went down to defeat, "like a row of ninepins," as
the *New York Times* so aptly described it. Goldwater
knew that he no longer had any choice in the matter. He

was deeply concerned that "private property is being abused and its concept being misguided by people who do not or will not understand that *human rights include property rights*. What protection does the individual have against a towering government which would take away his property rights?"[58] He went to Gettysburg to tell former President Eisenhower that he was going to vote against the Civil Rights Act. Then he returned to Washington to put his political life on the line.

The Republican convention was still a few weeks away. Twenty-eight of the 54 congressional supporters of Goldwater's candidacy were to vote *for* the Civil Rights Act.[59] Yet notwithstanding—with the eyes of the country, the Congress and the White House upon him—Goldwater took the floor of the Senate to deliver one of the most courageous speeches ever heard in the nation's capital. Even James Reston—no admirer of Goldwater—wrote that "the Senator's sincerity and depth of feeling . . . were perfectly obvious,"[60] as he told the Senate:

There have been few, if any, occasions when the searching of my conscience and the re-examination of my views of our constitutional system have played a greater part in the determination of my vote than they have on this occasion.

I am unalterably opposed to discrimination or segregation on the basis of race, color, or creed, or on any other basis; not only my words, but more importantly my actions through the years have repeatedly demonstrated the sincerity of my feeling in this regard.

This is fundamentally a matter of the heart. Our

problems of discrimination can never be cured by
laws alone; but I would be the first to agree that
laws can help—laws carefully considered and
weighed in an atmosphere of dispassion, in the absence of political demagoguery, and in the light of
fundamental constitutional principles.

For example, throughout my twelve years as a
member of the Senate Labor and Public Welfare
Committee, I have repeatedly offered amendments
to bills pertaining to labor that would end discrimination in unions, and repeatedly those amendments
have been turned down by the very members of
both parties who so vociferously support the
present approach to the solution of our problems.
Talk is one thing, action is another, and until the
members of the United States Senate and the people
of this country realize this, there will be no real
solution to the problem we face.

To be sure, a calm environment for the consideration of any law dealing with human relationships is
not easily attained—emotions run high, political
pressures become great, and objectivity is at a
premium. Nevertheless, deliberation and calmness
are indispensable to success.

It was in this context that I maintained high
hopes for this current legislation—high hopes that,
notwithstanding the glaring defects of the measure
as it reached us from the House of Representatives
and the sledgehammer political tactics which pro-
duced it, this legislation, through the actions of
what was once considered to be the greatest delib-
erative body on earth, would emerge in a form
both effective for its lofty purposes and acceptable
to all freedom-loving people.

It is with great sadness that I realize the non-fulfillment of these high hopes. My hopes were shattered when it became apparent that emotion and political pressure, not persuasion, not common sense, not deliberation, had become the rule of the day and of the processes of this great body.

One has only to review the defeat of commonsense amendments to this bill—amendments that would in no way harm it but would, in fact, improve it—to realize that political pressure, not persuasion or common sense, has come to rule the consideration of this measure.

I realize fully that the Federal government has a responsibility in the field of civil rights, but it would serve no purpose at this juncture to review my position as to just where that Federal responsibility appropriately lies. I supported the civil rights bills which were enacted in 1957 and 1960, and my public utterances during the debates on those measures and since reveal clearly the areas in which I feel that Federal responsibility lies and Federal legislation on this subject can be both effective and appropriate. Many of those areas are encompassed in this bill, and to that extent I favor it.

I wish to make myself perfectly clear. The two portions of this bill to which I have constantly and consistently voiced objections, and which are of such overriding significance that they are determinative of my vote on the entire measure, are those which would embark the Federal government on a regulatory course of action with regard to private enterprise in the area of so-called "public accommodations" and in the area of employment—to be more specific, Titles II and VII of the bill. I find no

constitutional basis for the exercise of Federal regulatory authority in either of these areas; and I believe the attempted usurpation of such power to be
a grave threat to the very essence of our basic system of government, namely, that of a constitutional
republic in which fifty sovereign states have re-
served to themselves and to the people those powers
not specifically granted to the central or Federal
government.

If it is the wish of the American people that the
Federal government should be granted the power
to regulate in these two areas and in the manner
contemplated by this bill, then I say that the Constitution should be so amended by the people as to
authorize such action in accordance with the procedures for amending the Constitution which that
great document itself prescribes. I say further that
for this great legislative body to ignore the Constitution and the fundamental concepts of our governmental system is to act in a manner which could
ultimately destroy the freedom of all American
citizens, including the freedoms of the very persons
whose feelings and whose liberties are the major
subject of this legislation.

My basic objection to this measure is, therefore,
constitutional. But, in addition, I would like to
point out to my colleagues in the Senate and to the
people of America, regardless of their race, color,
or creed, the implications involved in the enforce-
ment of regulatory legislation of this sort. To give
genuine effect to the prohibitions of this bill will
require the creation of a Federal police force of
mammoth proportions. It also bids fair to result in
the development of an "informer" psychology in

great areas of our national life—neighbors spying on neighbors, workers spying on workers, businessmen spying on businessmen, where those who would harass their fellow citizens for selfish and narrow purposes will have ample inducement to do so. These, the Federal police force and an "informer" psychology, are the hallmarks of the police state and landmarks in the destruction of a free society.

I repeat again: I am unalterably opposed to discrimination of any sort and I believe that though the problem is fundamentally one of the heart, some law can help—but not law that embodies features like these, provisions which fly in the face of the Constitution and which require for their effective execution the creation of a police state. And so, because I am unalterably opposed to the destruction of our great system of government and the loss of our God-given liberties, I shall vote "No" on this bill.

This vote will be reluctantly cast, because I had hoped to be able to vote "Yea" on this measure as I have on the civil rights bills which have preceded it; but I cannot, in good conscience to the oath that I took when assuming office, cast my vote in the affirmative. With the exception of Titles II and VII, I could wholeheartedly support this bill; but with their inclusion, not measurably improved by the compromise version we have been working on, my vote must be "No."

If my vote is misconstrued, let it be, and let me suffer its consequences. Just let me be judged in this by the real concern I have voiced here and not by words that others may speak or by what others may say about what I think.

My concern is not with this single legislative moment. My concern is not with a single faction of our citizens, no matter their power. My concern is with the fullness of this nation, with the fullness of freedom for everyone who lives in it and who will be born in it.

And I say that the general welfare must be spoken of now, despite the special appeals to special welfare. This is the time to attend to the liberties of all—not just to the demands of a few.

There is my concern. And this is where I stand.[61]

A Republican senator commented that Goldwater "saved his honor, but he may have lost the nomination."[62]

Hoping to capitalize on Goldwater's long-standing popularity with Southern conservatives, some Ku Klux Klan leaders ignored Goldwater's approval of nine of the eleven sections of the Civil Rights Act and declared they would support him for President. But early in August, Goldwater firmly repudiated the Klan, saying he didn't want the support of any organization bearing that name.[63]

At the Republican convention in San Francisco, Governor Scranton attempted to embarrass Goldwater by proposing that the convention affirm the constitutionality of the Civil Rights Act. However, he was flatly opposed by Rep. McCulloch of Ohio, who had played the key GOP role in passing the civil rights bill in the House. McCulloch felt that party conventions should not get into the business of saying whether a particular piece of legislation was or was not constitutional. What he considered far more important was to pledge enforce-

ment of the new civil rights law, and this plank Senator
Goldwater accepted.[64]

After the convention, the major civil rights leaders,
now fearful of a white backlash that would leave a
vengeful mark at the polls, signed a statement that denounced rioting and looting by Negroes "in several
urban areas", and urged their members to observe a
"broad curtailment if not total moratorium" on all mass
demonstrations until after the Presidential election.[65]
Except for an abortive traffic "stall-in" on the opening
day of the New York World's Fair (organized by the
Brooklyn chapter of CORE, which was suspended by
the parent organization for its pains)[66] the civil rights
leaders' control held up surprisingly well. Much as it
pained them to do so, the sit-in, phone-in, stall-in, chain-
in militants reluctantly reverted to civil obedience, at
least until November 3.

There was an air of almost eerie unreality about it
all—an unnatural calm, which seemed to be living on
borrowed time, at the whim and pleasure of Dr. Martin
Luther King.

For his own part, Senator Goldwater was as anxious
for racial calm as King and his supporters. As Theodore
H. White expressed it in *The Making of the President,
1964:*

It was Barry Goldwater who, on his own initiative
approached the President. . . . and volunteered to
eliminate entirely any appeal to passion of race in
the fall campaign, to which the President agreed in
private compact. In so doing, Goldwater yielded
certainly the strongest emotional appeal his cam-

paign might have aroused. Nor did he later, even in certain disaster, break his agreement.[67]

That Goldwater, of his own volition, made this crucial promise—and kept it—was one of the buried facts of the campaign. One can only hope it is not destined to become one of the buried pages of history.

THE CALIFORNIA
PRIMARY

As liberal Republicans envisioned it, the California primary was to be an updated version of the Gunfight at the OK Corral. Nelson Pureheart was to have it out once and for all with Bad Barry—finish the Senator off in a pitched primary battle and then walk off into the sunset with California's 86 convention votes in his hip pocket. It was a lovely liberal dream, but the Republican voters of California preferred to rewrite the scenario. And when the smoke had cleared, they had provided an OK for Senator Goldwater and a KO for Governor Rockefeller.

But this, of course, is getting ahead of our story. Perhaps it was just that, back in March, Republican liberals were still in a state of blissful hibernation, lulled to sleep by Joseph Alsop's written guarantee that "no serious Republican politician, even of the most Neanderthal type, any longer takes Goldwater seriously."[1] Perhaps it was not really until April that they got down to the serious business of counting convention delegates supporting

Goldwater, added two and two, and came up with the startling total of four. As *U.S. News & World Report* summarized it, "while opponents were winning headlines in primaries, Mr. Goldwater's men were fighting hundreds of little, unpublicized battles in precinct and county meetings, picking up one and two delegates at a time. . . . Senator Goldwater realized from the first that two-thirds of the states choose delegates in party conventions, not in primaries."[2]

Having completed their arithmetical calculations and arrived at conclusions that would have been readily apparent to a high school freshman, Republican liberals realized that California was the last chance—the only chance—to stop Goldwater before the convention. Accordingly, Rockefeller arrived in California with his aides, his image, and his checkbook, and the fight was on.

The California primary served as a sort of experimental laboratory for the coming Democratic campaign against Goldwater. The same smears—the same blatant appeal to fear—that had been incubated in the earlier primaries, now burst into full growth in the California campaign.

In the chapter on "Extremism", we have already seen how California Republican National Committeeman Joseph Martin, Jr., had announced he was supporting Rockefeller because Senator Goldwater was "the only candidate who is vigorously supported by the Birchers and the rightist lunatic fringe. Inevitably, his victory will also be their victory—their mandate to take over the party structure in its entirety."

The charge was kept red-hot in one of the most

widely publicized events of the campaign. Seven Republican legislators in California charged that "extremists" of the "radical right" were moving to seize control of the state GOP. Naturally, all seven were prospective members of Rockefeller's delegate-slate in the primary. In a joint statement, they claimed that the so-called radical rightists thought they had a "safe shelter in their acceptance by a respectable party leader, Senator Barry Goldwater."[3]

Rockefeller's supporters generally contented themselves with making blanket accusations intertwining Goldwater and extremism without deigning to name names. Joseph Martin, Jr., especially (who had by now become statewide coordinator for Rockefeller) preserved a lofty silence when challenged by the California Young Republicans to name the "extremists" he charged were heading their organization.[4]

The California Young Republicans' challenge went unanswered, but William Nelligan, the past president of the unofficial California Republican Assembly, did get down to specifics in one instance at least. Pointing to a list of contributors to a Goldwater dinner in March, Nelligan asserted that Goldwater supporters had appeared on the sponsoring committee of a dinner held the previous September for Robert Welch of the John Birch Society.[5]

Let us assume that Nelligan's information is correct in all respects. Was he seriously suggesting that at the height of a grueling make-or-break campaign Senator Goldwater's supporters should conduct an exhaustive investigation of every single supporter before deciding if his money was good? Had any of Goldwater's primary

opponents screened and scrutinized every single con-
tributor? Or Kennedy or Nixon in 1960? Or Eisenhower or Stevenson in 1952 or 1956? Or any other President or Presidential candidate in American history?

Much more to the point was what Nelligan did *not*
claim. He did *not* claim that the contributors in question
were part of Goldwater's campaign organization. He did
not claim that they were running for office, or in any
position of influence or power in the state GOP. He
did *not* claim that Goldwater had any association with
them.

For his own part, Rockefeller was satisfied simply to
make a noose out of the word "extremism" and then
loop it around Goldwater's neck. One of his recurring
themes was that a Goldwater victory would subject the
Republican party to the danger of control by "a narrow
extremism which fails to recognize the crucial need for
American leadership in the free world." Rockefeller
then proceeded to voice fear of the fear he had im-
planted in his listeners' minds, saying, "if this should
occur, I fear that the Republican Party . . . would wither
away like the Whigs, with disastrous consequences to
American democracy, based as it is upon the two-party
system."[6]

"Extremism" became the omnipresent stanza in Rockefeller's campaign repertoire. It was there in April when
Rockefeller referred to Goldwater and much of his California support and warned that if the California Republican party "follows the road of irresponsibility and
extremism, it cannot expect to command national attention."[7] It was there on June 1, the day before the primary
vote, when Rockefeller in a series of airport stops told

his audiences that Republican voters would choose between his sort of Republicanism—"constructive, for-
ward-looking, and responsible"—and that of Senator
Goldwater, which he called "narrow, doctrinaire extremism".[8]

One of Rockefeller's most influential supporters, Senator Thomas Kuchel, painted an even more frightening
picture, in this explosion of accusations:

> The Republican Party is facing one of the gravest
> dangers in its long history. . . . In California, all the
> odious totalitarian techniques of subversion and in-
> trigue are now being used by a frenetic but well-
> disciplined few to capture or control our party and
> to make it an antiquated implement of embittered
> obstruction.[9]

The *San Francisco Chronicle* noted that "at no time in
the speech did Kuchel mention the name of Senator
Barry Goldwater of Arizona. But references to Rockefeller's only rival in the June 2 California Primary were
scattered throughout the address."[10]

Ten days before, this same newspaper had leaped
headlong into the primary battle, with this page-one
charge:

> A rightist coalition, with John Birchers much in evi-
> dence, has set in motion an adroit plan to capture
> control of the Republican Party in California at
> both state and county levels.

Having set a Birchite bomb ticking in conservative
ranks, the *Chronicle* proceeded to detonate it in these

words: "Without fanfare, ultra-conservatives have entered candidates in 15 congressional elections, 5 Senate districts, and 38 Assembly races." The *Chronicle* conceded that their chances of victory were practically nil, but said that "the target of the rightists" was simply to win the Republican nomination in the primary.

The nomination carried with it a seat on the Republican State Central Committee, prompting the *Chronicle* to opine that the "rightists" would have a "solid bloc of 25 percent on the committee." Along with their allies already in the state group, the newspaper predicted that "the militants would wield powerful influence and in some cases control of the entire committee."[11]

Notice that the lead paragraph had "Birchers much in evidence", the second paragraph of the article spoke about "ultra-conservatives", whatever that was supposed to include, while the third paragraph referred not only to "militants" but to "rightists", knowing that every conservative considers himself to the right of center. This interchanging of all four terms inevitably had the effect of linking the entire conservative movement in California to the John Birch Society.

And the *Chronicle*, a very influential paper throughout California, wasn't through. In the most tortuous reasoning of the primary campaign, it groped its way through a five-step labyrinth, finally arriving at the name of Barry Goldwater. Quoting now from the *San Francisco Chronicle:*

Step 1: "The takeover plan—"
Step 2: "is being sparkplugged out of Southern California—"

Step 3: "where the Birch Society is strong—"
Step 4: "And extremist political activity is intense—"
Step 5: "and is finding strong outlet in the campaign
of Arizona Senator Barry Goldwater for the
Presidency."[12]

But *New York Times* reporter Wallace Turner flatly
refuted the entire accusation. Writing in the *New York
Times* near the end of the primary campaign, Turner
noted that GOP officials in California challenged the
whole idea that the "radical right" was about to devour
the Republican party. Turner was fully aware of the
wide national impression of an imminent takeover, and
was equally aware who had given the country that impression, laying it at the door of Rockefeller supporters
who sought "to present the Governor as the last bulwark of moderate Republicanism."

This *New York Times* reporter calmly went on to
say, "it is clear that the Radical Right does not control
the Republican Party of California, and the odds are that
it never will, even if Senator Goldwater should win the
Republican Primary and the Republican Presidential
nomination." He pointed out that since California is an
open-primary state, anyone can file for any office and
can become the party candidate if he wins the primary.
Thus, controlling the party committees did *not* mean
control of the nominations for public office. Then
Turner proceeded to debunk the idea that California was
becoming a satellite of the John Birch Society. He stated
that about a third of the vote in California was cast by
conservative Republicans of all stripes. The *New York
Times* reporter emphasized, however, that the "conservative Republicans in this 33 per cent are by no means

all of the Radical Right, which is small. *Its most 'ultra' members frequently are not even registered as Republicans.*" Finally, Turner stressed that while Goldwater was a conservative he was not an ultra.[13]

At this point, it will probably come as no surprise to the reader that this most illuminating article was buried on page 72 of the *New York Times* while the first article, alleging a plot to capture the California GOP, landed on page one of the *San Francisco Chronicle*.

Actually, the *San Francisco Chronicle* conceded that "no public statement of membership in San Francisco—or anywhere else, for that matter—has ever been given by [Birch] Society officers." However, the *Chronicle* stated that it had planted an undercover agent in the John Birch Society's San Francisco chapter. His exposé of membership was something less than electrifying. The paper disclosed that "the undercover agent's reports indicate that the San Francisco membership is 38—or a microscopic .005 per cent of the city's population."[14]

As of January 1, Republican registration in California had climbed up over the two and one-half million mark. But membership in *all* the California Republican organizations—official and unofficial alike—totaled only about 100,000, or about 4% of all California's Republican voters.[15] So, even if *all* the members of *all* the California Republican organizations had supported Goldwater, it would still have been only a drop in the bucket.

The campaign was marred by some unsavory incidents against various Rockefeller supporters, but these acts had no connection with the Goldwater campaign organization, and were in fact deplored by the Senator. Joseph Martin, Jr. complained to the Fair Campaign

Practices Committee that threatening phone calls were made to Rockefeller campaign headquarters in Los Angeles and in Santa Clara County, obscene calls to Rockefeller workers, and early-morning calls to voters urging them to vote for Rockfeller. In reply, John P. Vukasin, Jr., northern California chairman of the Goldwater campaign committee, said, "if those things happen, they're done by cranks. We've tried to avoid utilizing or capitalizing on this kind of thing. This is a cheap way to campaign. It's unworthy of California Republicans."[16]

One of the few incidents involving a Goldwater organization took place in San Diego, when the local Youth For Goldwater group picketed an appearance by Governor Rockefeller. A scuffle ensued, and in the disturbance a Rockefeller aide suffered a gash on his left arm when he was shoved into an urn. Two days later the chairman of the San Diego group resigned. The state chairman of Youth For Goldwater declared, "If he hadn't resigned, I would have asked for his resignation. We will not condone irresponsibility."[17]

But these were isolated incidents. The most bruising battle—first in the California primary, and then throughout the country—was the purely verbal one. And here the fight continued without let-up.

The fight took many forms and wore many faces. In an earlier chapter we have seen Rockefeller pounding away at the charge that a vote for Goldwater was a vote for the ultimate obliteration of the Social Security System. Another emotion-charged issue was the pending civil rights bill. Although the bill was not enacted into law until after the California primary, Goldwater left no doubt in anyone's mind of his opposition to it. He said

then—as he had said before, and would go on saying—
"it is my feeling that you cannot legislate civil rights."[18]
And with a courage that by now had become par for the
Goldwater course, he frankly announced his intention of
voting against the cloture motion to shut off debate on
the bill.[19] The *New York Times* wrote that "this stand
was reported to have cost him virtually the entire Negro
vote in California."[20]

The nuclear issue loomed large in the California primary campaign, and here as elsewhere Rockefeller glibly
misread and misquoted what Goldwater had said about
defoliating the forests along the border between North
and South Viet Nam. Here is what Goldwater actually
said in that now-famous interview on ABC-TV's "Issues
and Answers":

> There have been several suggestions made. *I don't
> think we would use any of them.* But defoliation of
> the forests by low-yield atomic weapons could well
> be done. When you remove the foliage, you re-
> move the cover.

These exact words appeared on page 36 of the *New
York Times* on May 25, 1964, but you would never
have known it to listen to Governor Rockefeller. A few
days later, in a speech at Santa Barbara, he said, "I do not
believe that the answer to the failures of the present
Administration is to be found in a reckless belligerence
typified by such *proposals* as . . . using nuclear weapons
to clear the jungles of Viet Nam."[21] For the New York
Governor, Goldwater's careful disavowal, "I don't think
we would use any of them," simply didn't exist.

And Rockefeller was equally oblivious of Goldwater's incisive foreign policy speech in Santa Barbara, California. Speaking at a luncheon in Santa Barbara at the end of May, Goldwater unequivocally stated, "our major objective must be to reduce Communist power to a level from which it cannot threaten our security or the peace, and of a foreign policy that could help preserve mean war. It means the alternative to war, a way to win the peace, to end threats to this nation, to its allies, to free nations everywhere, *without war*." Recalling the late John F. Kennedy's "firm resolution" in the Cuban missile crisis, Goldwater told his audience, "We cannot talk down the forward thrust of communist aggression. We cannot bluff them down. But we can face them down. And in the past we have done it. I say we can, and must do it again."[22]

There was nothing bellicose here. The talk was of peace, and of a foreign policy that could help preserve peace. But Rockefeller went right on depicting Goldwater in the most fear-ridden nuclear terms right up to Primary Day.

In a typical broadside, Rockefeller proclaimed that Goldwater's approach would heighten the danger of nuclear catastrophe.[23] And then came the Rockefeller forces' poison-pen letter about Goldwater and The Bomb. A mailing was sent out to *all* of California's registered Republicans entitled, *Who do you want in the room with the H-bomb?* A collection of Goldwater quotes lifted out of context, this single mailing cost an estimated $120,000.[24] The result was an unhappy one for Rockefeller. In Theodore H. White's words, "it had triggered a back reaction as much for its cost and size as for its shrill tone."[25] But the vicious, lashing charge it-self—the flogging of Goldwater as a nuclear know-nothing at best or madman at worst hung on long after the primary had ended. It followed the Senator from state to state throughout the Presidential campaign.

A week before the primary vote, radio and television stations up and down the state were broadcasting Rocke-feller announcements, ranging from 30-second radio taped dialogues with the Governor to five-minute tele-vision condensations of the biographical film, "The Rockefeller Story". On some stations the messages were scheduled almost hourly.[26] Neither side was giving out information about campaign expenditures, but the *New York Times* reported that "the Rockefeller outlay was authoritatively set by industry sources to be at least 10 times as big as the Goldwater campaign."[27] But as it developed, Rockefeller needed something more than a limitless checkbook to win support and influence voters.

Two days before the historic vote, James Reston was cautious if not a trifle queasy about the outcome. He wrote, "The polls say Mr. Rockefeller is going to win the last of the state primaries here in California on Tues-day, but the professional politicians swear that, even if the polls prove to be true, they are not going to nomi-nate him for the Presidency at San Francisco in July."[28]

Early in the campaign, Goldwater had made a speech in which he blamed Henry Cabot Lodge and Governor Nelson A. Rockefeller for the Republican party's defeat in the 1960 Presidential election. He was convinced that "if either—and preferably both—had worked half as hard as the rest of us did, Mr. Nixon would be in the White House today."[29]

Three weeks later, Rockefeller was asked point-blank if he could endorse Senator Goldwater as the party's nominee. The Governor replied that he would support the platform and the candidate his party nominated.[30] But Rockefeller refused to repeat the statement after Goldwater won the California primary. At a press conference the day after Goldwater's victory Rockefeller artfully side-stepped questions about supporting Goldwater. And as late as October Rockefeller was making the preposterous statement that his belief in a secret ballot prevented him from disclosing whether he would vote for Goldwater for President.[31]

Frank S. Meyer, a senior editor at *National Review*, wrote of the whole campaign for the Republican nomination: "The powers-that-be simply could not believe that [Goldwater] and the forces he represents were to be taken seriously. They were blinded by their own rhetoric, and rallied too late to present any stronger resistance than the farcical performance they put on at San Francisco."[32] Then, just as suddenly as it had started, the farce on the Republican left ended, and all over the country liberals of all stripes, shades, and hues mobilized for the coming atrocity, a knee-and-groin campaign that sought nothing less than the political entombment of Goldwater. What follows can only be considered a partial sampling of the torrent of abuse and vilification heaped daily upon Goldwater from the counting of the votes in the California primary till the final, frantic hours before Election Day on November 3. Some might call it the Decline and Fall of Political Reason—or call it "A Diary of Defamation".

A DIARY OF
DEFAMATION

JUNE 1*

If Milton Eisenhower was bluntly frank in Palm Springs, he warned ex-President Eisenhower that the nomination of Sen. Barry Goldwater would mean the end of the Republican Party, sending it to the same political boneyard already occupied by the Whigs and the Federalists. This is the opinion, at any rate, that the former President's most trusted brother is known to have voiced to others. (Joseph Alsop, *New York Herald Tribune*, p. 18.)

This was the latest variation on an old refrain. First, it was "Taft can't win"; then "Nixon can't win." In Goldwater's case, not only his defeat but the disintegration of the GOP was promised. It was so like the liberal Re-

---

* Unless otherwise indicated, the publication date of each quotation is the same as the date in bold type preceding the quotation.

publicans to take a walk when conservatives won—and then moan that Barry Goldwater was dividing the Republican party!

JUNE 7

In the *Pittsburgh Press* [there was] a statement from the Republican Congressman from Pittsburgh, Mr. James Fulton, in which he said he was not going to stand idly by and let the "kooks from Kooksville" dictate the policy of the Republican Party. He also made clear by this appellation that he was referring to Goldwater supporters. (Quoted in *Congressional Record* (unbound) June 10, 1964, p. 12695.)

In *The Making of the President, 1964,* Theodore H. White wrote: "There is not, and was not, anywhere in the entire high command, in the brains trust, or in the organizational structure of the Goldwater campaign, anyone who remotely qualified for the title 'kook'. Nor was there evident any 'kook' on the [convention] floor."[1]

JUNE 8

Governor Romney's statement said the Republican convention "will either take actions that will enable the party to provide the leadership the nation needs, or commence the suicidal destruction of the Republican party." (*New York Times*, p. 20).

Romney's choicest anti-Goldwater remarks furnished potent ammunition for the Democrats during the campaign, including a portion of at least one television commercial. If he realized how his speeches would later be used, he didn't seem to care; if he didn't realize it, he was sadly lacking in the most elementary political intelligence.

JUNE 10

The Board of Governors of the New York Young Republican Club approved a resolution last night opposing the candidacy of Senator Barry Goldwater for the Republican Presidential nomination. The resolution . . . said the club considered Mr. Goldwater . . . "potentially dangerous to the party and the nation." (*New York Times*, p. 32.)

As head of the Republican party in New York State, Governor Rockefeller could have scotched this resolution—or at least indicated his disapproval of its demagogic implications. His failure to say or do anything bore eloquent testimony to who it was that was dividing the Republican party.

JUNE 12

A Republican following this [Southern] strategy, especially against President Johnson, must mainly depend upon a single issue: the race issue. . . . The moderation Goldwater himself has thus far shown in discussing the race issue will not last long in a Presidential campaign. . . . For as the extent of normal Republican defections becomes more and more clear, the appeals to racial prejudice will automatically grow more and more shrill, overt and nasty. (Joseph Alsop, *New York Herald Tribune*, p. 20.)

In effect, Alsop—sitting as prosecutor, judge, and jury —was indicting Goldwater for racism in a kangaroo court before the Presidential campaign had even begun and assuming that the Senator was guilty until proven innocent. This, in spite of the fact that Goldwater had enjoyed great political popularity in the South as far back as 1960, the year he had voted *for* the second Civil Rights Act of the Eisenhower Administration. In spite of his vote for civil rights, considerable Southern delegate support made Goldwater a runner-up to Nixon at the 1960 Republican convention. In fact, even after Goldwater had asked that his name be withdrawn from consideration, ten members of the Louisiana delegation insisted upon voting for him nonetheless.[2]

JUNE 13

"I've come here to offer our party a real choice," [Scranton] declared. "I reject the echo we have thus far been handed—the echo of fear and of reaction, the echo from the never-never land that puts our nation on the road backward to a lesser place in the world of free men . . ." He called on his party to unite "behind our traditional principles and not behind some weird parody of our real beliefs." (*New York Times*, p. 1.)

JUNE 14

Before the convention, [Governor Scranton said]

that the party had reached the "ludicrous point where every responsible leader knows that to stave off defeat in November, a make-believe coating of moderation must be shellacked over the views that have been uttered by the present front-runner." Pleading for liberal Republicanism, Mr. Scranton remarked that a "small but vocal minority has too often made our party sound naive, irresponsible, reactionary, and heartless." (*New York Times*, p. 42.)

A year after his defeat, Goldwater commented, "Rockefeller and Scranton cut me up so bad there was no way on God's green earth that we could have won. I knew it the day after the convention."[3]

JUNE 15

A confidential eight-page memorandum being circulated to leading Republican moderates and liberals asserts that if Senator Barry Goldwater is nominated for President, he probably would lose every state except Arizona, and "would bring on wholesale slaughter of the Republican Party." The memorandum, prepared by the Ripon Society ... urged that in a four-week campaign to defeat the Arizona Senator, "Goldwater's weaknesses should be exploited mercilessly." [The Ripon Society memorandum stated,] "The Goldwater 'Don't wreck the Party' line must be refuted. This is simply a tactic to consolidate the Goldwater lead." (*New York Times*, p. 21.)

The Ripon Society appeared to be the liberals' Trojan

Horse in the Republican party. In their arrogant disregard of the political consequences of their memorandum, it was not difficult to see who was willing to "bring on the wholesale slaughter of the Republican Party".

JUNE 15

The fact of the matter is that Scranton thinks the Republican Party is very likely to follow the Whig and the Federalist parties into oblivion if Goldwater is the 1964 Presidential nominee. (Joseph Alsop, *New York Herald Tribune*, p. 18.)

In reading this re-run of Alsop's June 1 column, one is reminded of Edgar Allan Poe's story about "premature burial". In this instance, the GOP body was not only alive, but pulsating with activity. This in no way inhibited Alsop, however, in his efforts to lower it into the ground.

JUNE 16

"Most of us know that in this troubled world, we need an American foreign policy that thinks from the head, not one that shoots from the hip," the Governor [Scranton] said. . . . "This is not the hour for us to join those extreme reactionaries who are anything but conservative—those radicals of the right who would launch a system of dime-store feudalism that is foreign to these shores and foreign to the American way of thinking." (*New York Times*, p. 25.)

JUNE 20

[Scranton said that] Senator Goldwater would take the party down "the low road into the dusty limbo of minority politics." (*New York Times*, p. 14.)

After the convention Scranton made a great many speeches in Goldwater's behalf in Illinois, Minnesota, Iowa, and Pennsylvania. *National Review* wrote that his speeches "included the apparently sincere belief that Goldwater would make a good President".[4] But whether the pro-Goldwater Scranton of September and October ever successfully refuted the anti-Goldwater Scranton of June and July is dubious to say the least.

JUNE 20

Governor Wallace of Alabama will no longer be needed as a collector of the white "protest" vote, North or South. Senator Goldwater will suffice for those seeking a states rights' standard to repair to. Perhaps this is one of the "consequences" of his civil rights vote that the Senator was willing to "suffer." (*New York Times*, p. 24.)

The *New York Times*' own Washington columnist, James Reston, took a different view. The day before, he had written that Goldwater's decision to vote against the civil rights bill "may very well have strengthened those who oppose his nomination as the Republican Presidential candidate."[5]

JUNE 22

In his extreme views on states' rights, [Goldwater] is in fact one who would dissolve the Federal union into a mere confederation of the states. . . . he would nullify if he could the central purpose of the Civil War amendments, and would take from the children of the emancipated slaves the protection of the national union. (Walter Lippmann, *Newsweek*, p. 19.)

Goldwater's reverence for the Constitution had been an integral part of many speeches and statements and had never before been called into question, even by his bitterest political foes. He voted against the 1964 Civil Rights Act because he could find "no constitutional basis for the exercise of Federal regulatory authority" in the areas of employment and public accommodations.

JUNE 22

It is a commentary on the plight of those determined to remain party-line Republicans today that in the end they will have to wrap themselves in the American flag and hope for national disaster. Rout for the Americans in Southeast Asia, race conflict in the United States, death or incapacitation of the American president—this is the nightmarish stuff that Right-wing dreams are made of. And even these catastrophes might not be enough to elect Barry Goldwater. (*The New Leader*, p. 3.)

It may amaze the reader, as it did the author, to learn that this vilification of Senator Goldwater was written by a fellow Republican, George F. Gilder, formerly editor of the now defunct *Advance*, a liberal Republican journal. Such was the nightmarish stuff that left-wing Republican dreams were made of—a crippling defeat for Barry Goldwater whatever the cost to the party!

JUNE 24

If elected, Mr. Goldwater could very well be the *last* President of the United States. (*Christian Century*, p. 847.)

Small wonder that *The Living Church*, an independent magazine for Episcopalians, said editorially in reference to anti-Goldwater attacks: "It seems to be the latest fad among the American clergy who glory in the title of 'liberal' to vie with one another in skills of the game which they used to call 'character assassination' when Joe McCarthy was flourishing. We earnestly hope that this kind of liberal bigotry will not become standard fare in the pulpits of the Episcopal, or any other, church."[6]

JUNE 26

[Scranton has] run head on, into the hard fact that stopping Senator Barry Goldwater means changing the minds of Goldwater delegates whose minds are seldom accessible to reason, because so many of them are fanatics. (Joseph Alsop, *New York Herald Tribune*, p. 16.)

A more rational analysis was made by Vermont Royster, writing in the *Wall Street Journal:* "Far from being the crackpots of the stereotype images, the supporters of Senator Goldwater are mostly lawyers, doctors, small businessmen, farmers and white collar workers, with a sprinkling of those from the more skilled labor groups. . . . The secret of Senator Goldwater, if that's the word for it, is simply that he speaks for this somewhat amorphous middle class."[7]

JUNE 30

The new Goldwater party is being born in the midst of the national crisis over Negro rights, and it is impossible to doubt that Sen. Goldwater intends to make his candidacy the rallying point of the white resistance. (Walter Lippmann, *New York Herald Tribune,* p. 18.)

Three weeks later, Lippmann was purring, "Sen. Goldwater has shown a commendable distaste for identifying himself with the white backlash."[8] Proving that saints can be quoted against each other—and even themselves!

JULY 4

Mr. [Roy] Wilkins added later that in his opinion "any man who rejects the use of law to settle problems can only condone violence." This remark presumably referred to Senator Goldwater who voted against the Senate closure and against the Civil Rights Bill. (*New York Times,* p. 4.)

There was a grim humor in this clear inference that Barry Goldwater—who would make a campaign issue of "violence in the streets"—was condoning racial violence on either side.

JULY 6

Set speeches to large rallies of the already-converted were the Goldwater rule in California. He broke the rule just once. . . . The occasion was the television interview in the course of which the Senator blithely suggested nuclear defoliation as one possible way to win the Vietnamese war. (Joseph Alsop, *New York Herald Tribune*, p. 14.)

Senator Goldwater had personally suggested nothing of the kind, as we have seen. In spite of Goldwater's disavowals, however, one of the wire services carried a story declaring that Senator Goldwater had "proposed" the use of low-yield atomic weapons to defoliate the forests along the borders of South Viet Nam. A month and a half later Alsop was still blithely misquoting the Senator; and as late as October 5, the *New York Times* was sputtering in righteous rage about "the airiness with which he discussed the possible use of atomic weapons to 'defoliate' Communist supply trails in Viet Nam."[9]

JULY 9

In foreign affairs [Goldwater] . . . is ready to confront the Soviet Union and China with a choice between capitulation and war. (Walter Lippmann, *New York Herald Tribune*, p. 18.)

Months later, Mr. Lippmann blandly inquired: "Does anybody say that Barry Goldwater wants a war? I know of no one who says it, or thinks it."[10]

JULY 9

"We must ask ourselves," [Scranton] continued, "what events [Goldwater] is looking forward to, to improve his chances in the South. Tragically, there can be but one explanation. He, or those close to him, hope to gain by racial unrest. Are they looking forward to the possibility of human relations being put to the torch and the hope of finding votes in the backlash?" (*New York Times*, p. 19.)

A week before, the *New York Times* had noted in a front-page story, "Senator Barry Goldwater is seriously disturbed that racial tensions may become an explosive issue in the Presidential campaign. . . . The Arizona Senator is thinking of calling a meeting of some religious and academic figures plus his own political advisers, to suggest to him how he could keep race from being a campaign issue. . . . Although what he regards as the subterranean issue of the white backlash, or resentment over Negro militancy, may help him, he would never exploit this. He simply thinks the issue is too dangerous."[11]

JULY 9

Ambassador Lodge hammered hard in his testimony [before the Republican Platform Committee in San Francisco] at irresponsibility in foreign pol-

icy—an indirect but plain attack on Senator Goldwater. "We must never countenance such a thing
as a trigger-happy foreign policy," Mr. Lodge said,
"which would negate everything we stand for and
destroy everything we hope for—including life itself." (*New York Times*, p. 18.)

For any so obtuse as to miss the identity of Mr. Trigger Happy, the *New York Times* could be counted
upon to supply the subtitle: "an indirect but plain attack
on Senator Goldwater".

JULY 12

William Chester, an official of the International
Longshoremen's and Warehousemen's Union . . .
charged that "Senator Goldwater has become a
rallying point for all the racists in America, such as
the Ku Klux Klan, White Citizens Councils, and
others." (*New York Times*, p. 58.)

A month before, Senator Goldwater had endorsed a
public accommodations bill in Phoenix, Arizona, that
would prohibit public businesses from refusing service
because of race, color, or creed.[12]

JULY 13

Senator Goldwater has decided not to take a post-
convention vacation in Germany. One reason was a
Columbia Broadcasting System news report yesterday that asserted Mr. Goldwater's trip signaled a
link between the "right wing of the United States

and that of Bavaria. . . ." Goldwater called this "the damndest lie I ever heard." (*New York Times*, p. 18.)

This charge by CBS was reproduced in one of Governor Scranton's campaign tabloids. Five days later, the *New York Times* carried this "clarifying statement" broadcast by the CBS News correspondent, Daniel Schorr: "In speaking the other day of a move by Senator Goldwater to link up with these forces, I did not mean to suggest a conscious effort on his part *of which there is no proof here*, but rather a process of gravitation which is visible here."[18] The author considers it highly unlikely that the "clarifying statement" ever caught up with the smear, or clarified anything where it did.

JULY 13

Gov. William W. Scranton [sent Senator Goldwater] a letter that was largely a scalding attack on his rival for the Presidential nomination. . . . Mr. Scranton made such charges as these: "You have too often casually prescribed nuclear war as a solution to a troubled world. . . . Goldwaterism has come to stand for refusing to stand for law and order in maintaining racial peace. . . . In short, Goldwaterism has come to stand for a whole crazy-quilt collection of absurd and dangerous positions that would be soundly repudiated by the American people in November." (*New York Times*, pp. 1, 18.)

Theodore H. White wrote: ". . . the letter and the weekend seeking of confrontation ground . . . made the

Republican convention the stage for the destruction of
the leading Republican candidate. What Rockefeller had
begun in spring, Scranton finished in June and at the
convention; the painting for the American people of a
half-crazed leader indifferent to the needs of American
society at home, and eager to plunge the nation into war
abroad."[14]

JULY 14

[Roy Wilkins of the NAACP said,] "Those who
say that the doctrine of ultra-conservatism offers
no menace should remember that a man came out
of the beer halls of Munich, and rallied the forces
of Rightism in Germany. All the same elements are
there in San Francisco now." (*New York Times*, p.
30.)

The day before, Senator Goldwater had told Southern delegates to the Republican convention that segregation was "wrong morally, and in some instances, con-
stitutionally." He said he would enforce the Civil Rights
Act and use the "moral power" of the Presidency to
help end discrimination.[15]

JULY 15

[William] Miller is a Catholic. The white backlash
is particularly strong among lower income Poles,
Irish, Italians, and other predominantly Catholic
racial groups. If a fellow Catholic is placed on the
Republican ticket, his appeal to these groups will
no doubt strengthen the backlash tendency. (Joseph Alsop, *New York Herald Tribune*, p. 22.)

There was, of course, one Grand-Canyon-sized hole in Alsop's diatribe: Bill Miller had been recorded *for* the Civil Rights Act of 1964.

JULY 15

Senator Barry Goldwater has been in correspondence with the Sudeten-German leader, Hans Christoph Seebohm. . . . Competent informants said today that Mr. Goldwater and Mr. Seebohm, who is Transport Minister in Chancellor Ludwig Erhard's Cabinet, had been in "frequent and friendly" correspondence for some time. . . . Mr. Seebohm was chastised by Chancellor Erhard last month after . . . he asserted that the Munich Agreement of 1938 remained a legally binding compact. (*New York Times*, p. 21.)

Three days later, the *New York Times* had to report that "Hans Christoph Seebohm denied today that he had been in friendly correspondence with Senator Barry Goldwater." A spokesman for Seebohm made it abundantly clear that Seebohm had "never seen, never spoken to, and never exchanged letters with Senator Goldwater." In explanation to its readers, the *New York Times* could only offer this feeble statement: ". . . the report was based on information from competent sources known to be informed of Dr. Seebohm's interest in the conservative movement in the United States."[16] Apparently it never occurred to these champions of "all the news that's fit to print" that the most competent source of information about Senator Goldwater's activities was Senator Goldwater himself.

JULY 16

[Walter Reuther, president of the United Auto Workers, said,] "What happened at San Francisco was a tragedy. In this crucial period, the election of Goldwater as President would be a catastrophe. The whole free-world alliance would disintegrate for lack of confidence." [Norman Thomas, the Socialist leader, said,] "I think the Republican Party platform plus Goldwater is a prescription for World War III." (*New York Times*, p. 19.)

Reuther had considered it little less than catastrophic when Goldwater was re-elected to the Senate six years before. As for the octogenarian Thomas, there was very little meaningful right-wing activity that he did *not* consider "a prescription for World War III".

JULY 16

It is quite evident in the platform that Sen. Goldwater is relying heavily on attracting Democrats from the white backlash. . . . [Goldwater] appears to be gambling recklessly on racism and jingoism. (Walter Lippmann, *New York Herald Tribune*, p. 20.) Today in the same city of San Francisco, the party of the same President Lincoln is sorely divided over the continued emancipation of the Negro. (Drew Pearson, *New York Post*, p. 29.)

It became more and more apparent that to Pearson and Lippmann anyone to the right of Martin Luther King was a racist. With lofty disdain they ignored the

civil rights plank in the 1964 Republican platform, which
called for "full implementation and faithful execution"
of *all* civil rights laws.

JULY 17

[Scranton] told the sparse airport audience that
greeted his arrival in San Francisco that he would
continue his anti-Goldwater fight to keep the
G.O.P. from becoming "another name for some
ultra-rightist society". (*Time*, p. 19.)

This was Scranton's swan song as a Presidential candidate. But as he must have realized, these dissonant notes
would linger on, right up to Election Day.

JULY 17

[If Goldwater becomes President] the abolition of
the Health, Education and Welfare Department is
bound to be given serious consideration. But one
can foresee that, pending a final decision, this department will be confided to the safe-and-sure
hands of Robert Welch—provided he does not
consider that heading the John Birch Society is a
higher duty. (Joseph Alsop, *New York Herald
Tribune*, p. 16.)

It was this sort of "jocular" reporting that had moved
the distinguished political columnist Ruth Montgomery
to write: "the manner in which the so-called liberal press
has been striking for the jugular of . . . Barry Goldwater

is about as sportsmanlike as a trip to Dachau under Hitler."[17]

JULY 17

[Governor Romney] said he would support the national campaign only if it progressed in a "responsible manner, free of hate-peddling and fear-spreading." (*New York Times*, p. 12.)

That Goldwater made no racist appeals is a matter of public record. But in one of their rare face-to-face meetings after the convention—notwithstanding Goldwater's announced support of Romney's bid for re-election—the Governor twice refused to endorse Goldwater's candidacy.[18]

JULY 18

[Governor Brown of California stated] that the Senator's acceptance speech had "the stench of Fascism." (*New York Times*, p. 6.)

JULY 19

Gov. Edward T. Breathitt [of Kentucky] charged the Republicans "expelled tolerance and compassion and common sense" from the party during their national convention. "The extremists at San Francisco carried out—as coolly as a butcher would carve a roast—the most extensive political purge since the Moscow trials and the Nazi purge of 1934," said the Governor. (*New York Times*, p. 53.)

JULY 19

Mayor James V. Diprete Jr. of Cranston [R.I.], a Republican, called Senator Barry Goldwater today a "fascist who is threatening to take over this country by dividing the American people against one another. . . ." Mayor Diprete said, "I'm convinced that Mr. Goldwater is a fanatic who is deluded by some sort of a messianic complex that he is the lord and savior of the U.S., and I'm also convinced that he is willing to see the country provoked to any extreme to accomplish his goal." (*New York Times*, p. 57.)

The rantings of Governors Brown and Breathitt were the predictable Pavlovian responses of Democratic hacks exposed to the stimuli of anything Republican and worse still—conservative. As for the Mayor of Cranston, R.I., one can only wonder if he would have been quoted in the *New York Times* if he had *not* denounced Senator Goldwater. In any case, this kamikaze attack on Mr. Conservative was a lurid preview of the campaign Bruce L. Felknor, executive director of the Fair Campaign Practices Committee, was to call "the most vicious and bitter I've ever seen, or for that matter, heard tell of."[19]

JULY 19

I now believe I know how it felt to be a Jew in Hitler's Germany. . . . Barry Goldwater, at best, is

a hopeless captive of the lunatic, calculating right-
wing extremists. . . . a challenge must be issued to
the Negro people . . . [to] ensure that Goldwaterism and extremism and anti-Negroism will be so
brutally defeated that they can never again threaten
the future of America. (Jackie Robinson, *New
York Herald Tribune*, p. 15.)

To Jackie Robinson, extremism in pursuit of Goldwater was clearly no vice.

JULY 24

According to the Lodge forces, the Goldwater-
dominated Republican National Committee stopped
opening mail from rank-and-file Republicans more
than a week ago, because it was running 3 to 1
against Goldwater. That statistic has the ring of
truth to it. (*Commonweal*, p. 495.)

To the virulently anti-conservative *Commonweal*,
anything running three to one against Goldwater had
"the ring of truth to it".

JULY 27

Canon John Collins, former chairman of the British
Campaign for Nuclear Disarmament . . . called on
his fellow churchmen, including the Archbishop of
Canterbury and the Pope, to condemn the policies
of Senator Barry Goldwater. Today he asked:
"How long will we remain silent or passive in face

of the growing resurgence of the fascist mentality?" (*New York Times*, p. 28.)

This same article gave a significant clue to the Canon's own mentality: in a sermon in St. Paul's Cathedral
he declared that capitalism was incompatible with the
Christian gospel.

AUGUST

A victorious Goldwater and his extremist supporters would speedily make life all but unbearable for
unions, for working people, for the poor. (*COPE
Newsletter*, New York State AFL-CIO.)

The union bosses undoubtedly considered "unbearable"
the *mot juste* for the bill Goldwater had introduced in
1963 that would have given workers a chance to veto a
strike through a secret-ballot vote conducted by the
NLRB. Another provision of this bill would have out-
lawed the "union shop" except where a state had laws—
or enacted laws—to permit such labor contracts.[20]

AUGUST 2

Representative James Roosevelt, Democrat of California, said today that Senator Barry Goldwater
was trying to reshape the Republican party into
"the image of the John Birch Society" and into the
pattern "of political parties in totalitarian coun-
tries." (*New York Times*, p. 49.)

Months later the *St. Louis Globe Democrat* reminded
its readers that "Mr. Goldwater is not a member of the

John Birch Society, and has not solicited their vote."[21] Two simple facts—but the most acute political radar would have been hard put to find them in more than one or two other major papers.

AUGUST 7

You can usually expect the right-wing "anti-communists" of the McCarthyite or Goldwater stripe to vote "no" on genuinely anti-communist legislation if it costs money, even legislation aimed at strengthening the military establishment. . . . Goldwaterism in foreign affairs has a militarist, xenophobic and virulently anti-communist flavor which closely parallels the views of fascist and crypto-fascist movements everywhere. (*Commonweal*, pp. 530, 533.)

These frenzied fantasies ignored Goldwater's strong support for NATO and his vote for increased spending on manned bombers. Even his much-maligned acceptance speech before the Republican convention envisioned "a day when all the Americas, North and South, will be linked in a mighty system, a system in which the errors and misunderstandings of the past will be submerged, one by one in a rising tide of prosperity and interdependence."[22]

AUGUST 7

Dear Mr. Robinson:

If I were to term you a bigot and a menace to our country you would resent it, I am sure, and resent it mostly because I would make the statement without ever having done you the courtesy of visiting with you to discuss your views. Yet you have attacked me rather viciously on several occasions without ever having done me the courtesy to call and say—let's sit down and see just where you stand on these various issues.

From the venomous attacks leveled at me by some members of the press and even some members of our own party, I can't rightly blame you for holding these views, but because you occupy a place of prominence in our citizenry, your remarks aren't just the remarks of somebody else. I would deem it a great pleasure to sit down and break bread with you sometime to give me the opportunity to explain my life-long feeling in the field of civil rights and to give you the chance to interrogate me further on them and other issues. If you are inclined to say yes, let me know, and I am sure we can set up a date to our mutual satisfaction.

Sincerely,
Barry Goldwater

Dear Senator Goldwater:

Relating to your proposal that we discuss civil rights, what could you possibly have to say?

. . . . Are you going to tell me why you have consistently attacked the constitutionality of the United States Supreme Court edict on schools?

. . . . Are you going to tell me what constituted your genuine motive in voting against the civil rights bill? Did you really believe certain sections to be unconstitutional or did you and do you feel that it presented an opportunity to capitalize on anti-civil-rights reaction, North and South?

Are you going to tell me why you have allowed yourself to become a political bedfellow with some of the slimiest elements in the nation, such as the Ku Klux Klan and the John Birch Society?

. . . . Are you going to tell me the whole story about the withdrawal of Governor Wallace?

. . . . I am working to help strengthen the thrust of Republicans for Johnson, Independents for Johnson, and any and every freedom-loving, extremism-defying movement which will help to insure the farce of San Francisco shall not engulf our nation in a long nightmare of hopelessness and havoc and holocaust.

If in view of these questions which I raise in absolute sincerity and conviction you still think a meeting between us would be fruitful, I am available at your convenience.

Sincerely yours,
Jackie Robinson
(*New York Herald Tribune*, p. 4.)

Goldwater's letter to Jackie Robinson was written on July 25. The day before—again quoting Theodore H. White—"it was Barry Goldwater who, on his own initiative, approached the President at the height of the rioting, and volunteered to eliminate entirely any appeal to passion of race in the Fall campaign, to which the President agreed in private compact. In so doing, Goldwater yielded certainly the strongest emotional appeal his campaign might have aroused. Nor did he later, even in certain disaster, break his agreement."[23] Robinson asked, "what could you possibly have to say?" It would have been easy enough to find out. But to have the

meeting first, and publish his conclusions *later*—to hear
Goldwater out, and decide on a course of action *after-
ward*—would have required qualities of fairness and
courage that Robinson had apparently left behind him
on the ball field.

AUGUST 8

[AFL-CIO President George] Meany said on the
views of Sen. Barry Goldwater, the GOP Presidential nominee: "I think he feels the country would
be better off, if we didn't have trade unions."
(*AFL-CIO News*, p. 1.)

As far back as 1960, in *The Conscience of a Conservative*, Goldwater had written: "I believe that unionism,
kept within its proper and natural bounds, accomplishes a
positive good for the country. Unions *can* be an instru-
ment for achieving economic justice for the working
man."[24] Nothing Goldwater had said or written before or
since had altered these views.

AUGUST 10

State Dept. experts have been trying to figure out
just what connection, if any, there is among the
American election, the argument between Moscow
and Peking, and the deliberate attack on U.S. destroyers in the Gulf of Tonkin. Only conclusion
the experts can reach is that the Goldwater candidacy is duck soup for the Red Chinese. It fits in
exactly with their thesis that you can't get along

with the Western World. (Drew Pearson, *New York Post*, p. 25.)

Using the same twisted reasoning, Winston Churchill would have been blamed for World War II.

AUGUST 13

One of the two parties has been taken over by fanatics who at the convention showed no inclination to be magnanimous in victory. . . . [Barry Goldwater] is at home at the very border of absurdity. . . . A type of primitivism has emerged and is gaining a still unmeasured mass support. (Max Ascoli, *The Reporter*, p. 27.)

To the Max Ascolis of this world anyone who is genuinely conservative is a fool or a lunatic or a fascist, or more likely a combination of the three. From his fantasy-hedged vantage point, conservatism per se has evolved into "primitivism".

AUGUST 15

The presidential candidacy of Sen. Barry Goldwater poses a "menace" to the future of "free American trade unionism" . . . Steelworkers Pres. David J. McDonald declared. . . . McDonald makes the following points: A vote for Goldwater would mean destruction of the USWA [United Steelworkers of America]. "If you want to save your union, if you want to continue to have a strong United Steelworkers of America, then I urge you

by all the powers of good to go out and support
Lyndon B. Johnson for President of the United
States." (*AFL-CIO News*, p. 1.)

This frightening portrayal of wage slavery under a
Goldwater Administration was in the text of a ten-
minute political action film to be shown at local union
meetings and "wherever else possible".

AUGUST 15

[At the Montana AFL-CIO convention,] topping
the list of guest speakers was Undersecretary of
Labor John F. Henning, who ripped into Goldwater's anti-labor record. He suggested that if
Goldwater and his backers can be taken literally in
their public positions, the implication of forced
labor camps to solve unemployment problems
would not be inconsistent. (*AFL-CIO News*, p.
3.)

At times such as this it seemed as if the campaign had
lost all meaning and had become instead a surrealistic
nightmare.

AUGUST 30

[Goldwater's] first talk after he was nominated
condemned violence in the streets, and most ob-
servers read that as a reference to Negro demonstrations. Last week, speaking of disorder, Senator
Goldwater told his listeners at the Illinois State Fair
in Springfield that their wives and daughters would

know what he meant. "I don't have to quote statistics," the Senator said, "for you to know what I mean. You know. You have to face it every day on the front page or the back page of your paper. Every wife and mother—yes, every woman and girl—knows what I mean, knows what I'm talking about." The appeal to racial fear was not misunderstood. (*New York Times*, Section IV, p. E3.)

One of the earliest references to street violence in the campaign was made by former President Eisenhower in his address to the Republican convention at San Francisco. Eisenhower cautioned, "Let us not be guilty of maudlin sympathy for the criminal who, roaming the streets with switchblade knife and illegal firearms seeking a helpless prey, suddenly becomes upon apprehension a poor, underprivileged person who counts upon the compassion of our society and the laxness or weakness of too many courts to forgive his offense."[25] Senator Goldwater was in total agreement with Eisenhower on this point—and it was not suggested then, or later, that racism had motivated the ex-President's speech. Actually Senator Goldwater *had* quoted statistics almost three weeks before this article appeared. Speaking on the floor of the Senate, Goldwater stated: "The *New York Times*, in its July 21 issue, noted that major crime rose 10 percent in the United States in 1963 . . . youths under 18 accounted for 50.4 percent of the arrests in suburban areas for serious crimes. Juveniles made up 63.4 percent of those arrested for auto theft, 51 percent of those arrested for burglary, and 50 percent of those arrested for larceny."[26] There was obviously nothing racist about these crime statistics or the source from which the Senator drew them.

SEPTEMBER 1

IS BARRY GOLDWATER PSYCHOLOGICALLY FIT TO BE PRESIDENT OF THE UNITED STATES?

1,846 psychiatrists answer this question in the next issue of *Fact* magazine. What do psychiatrists think of Goldwater's fitness to keep his finger on the atomic trigger? Of his tendency to view issues and people from extremes, as either all good or all bad? Of his veneration of the military, his aversion to compromise, his mistrust of strangers and the impulsive statements he later modifies or denies?

What do psychiatrists say about Mr. Goldwater's belief that our only choice is between complete surrender to Communism and atomic war? What facts concerning his medical history are pertinent to his candidacy? Does Mr. Goldwater appear overly suspicious or overly belligerent?

The answers to all these questions are contained in a 64-page psychological study of Barry Goldwater in the next issue of *Fact*. In making this study, the editors of *Fact* polled every psychiatrist in the nation, using a list of names supplied by the American Medical Association. Over a quarter of a million words of professional opinion were received. Never before has a political figure been the subject of such an intensive character analysis. (From a full-page ad in the *New York Times*, September 15, 1964, p. 23.)

Ralph Ginzburg, publisher of *Fact* magazine, revealed that the magazine had allocated $100,000 to run this ad in major newspapers across the country.[27]

On July 24, 1964—one week after Barry Goldwater received the Republican nomination—*Fact* magazine had sent out a questionnaire to all of the country's 12,356 psychiatrists. Enclosed with the questionnaire was a letter which read:

Dear Doctor:

Do you think that Barry Goldwater is psychologically fit to serve as President of the United States? ...

A recent survey by Medical Tribune showed that psychiatrists—in sharp contrast to all other M.D.'s—hold Goldwater in low esteem. Among M.D.'s generally, approximately two thirds prefer Goldwater over Johnson, but among psychiatrists, the preference is for Johnson by 10 to 1 ...

Note that the enclosed questionnaire has no special provisions for your name or your address. You may add them if you wish or remain anonymous.

Enclosed is a reply envelope, for which no stamp is required. Your prompt reply will be appreciated. We believe the findings of this survey will receive much attention in the press, and will weigh heavily in the choice made by the American electorate.

With gratitude, cordially,
Warren Borosson
Managing Editor[28]

In a joint letter to *Fact*, the president and medical director of the American Psychiatric Association wrote:

"By attaching the stigma of extreme political partisanship to the psychiatric profession as a whole in the heated climate of the current political campaign, *Fact* has in effect administered a low blow to all who would advance the treatment and care of the mentally ill of America."[29]

Fact magazine claimed that the American Medical Association had "supplied" the names for the survey. But the Association denied this, saying that the names had been supplied by a New Jersey concern that dealt in mailing lists.[30] The president of the American Medical Association assailed the article as "an exercise in yellow journalism and scientific irresponsibility". In a withering critique he pointed out that "if *Fact's* figures are accurate, 89 percent of the nation's psychiatrists did not receive the questionnaire or did not choose to participate. Those who replied to the questionnaire were not required to sign their names. No scientist or statistician would take such a survey seriously or give any credence to the results."[31]

Since the respondents were not required to sign their names, anyone at all—doctor, patient, nurse or scrubwoman—could have filled out the questionnaire and returned it unsigned to *Fact* magazine.

The full-page ad for *Fact* stated that "1,846 psychiatrists answer this question [as to Goldwater's psychological fitness] in the next issue of *Fact* magazine." But actually, *Fact* printed excerpts from only 163 letters, of which 61 were "anonymous".

One of the unsigned letters—from a "board-certified psychiatrist"—read:

"I believe Goldwater is grossly psychotic. His statements reveal a serious thinking disorder. . . . He is grandiose, which is suggestive of delusions of grandeur. He is suspicious, suggestive of paranoia. He is impulsive, suggesting that he has poor control over his feelings and that he acts on angry impulses. This alone would make him *extremely* psychologically unfit to serve as President. A President must not act on impulse!

But in addition, he *consciously* wants to destroy the world with atomic bombs. He is a mass-murderer at heart and a suicide. He is amoral and immoral. A dangerous lunatic! . . .

P.S. Any psychiatrist who does not agree with the above is himself psychologically unfit to be a psychiatrist."[32]

A much more temperate view was contained in this perceptive letter signed by William R. Reid, M.D., of Tulsa, Oklahoma. Dr. Reid wrote:

"If most psychiatrists do not prefer Goldwater, it is certainly no surprise. Psychiatrists have a strong tendency to be 'do-gooders' and are therefore more politically liberal. Since I am a practicing psychiatrist, I feel free to criticize my profession. Among M.D.'s we are the most psychologically disturbed of the group. This is what motivates us to be interested in other people's problems."[33]

Another of those buried facts of the campaign was revealed by Fulton Lewis, Jr., in a radio broadcast on August 3, 1964. Lewis revealed that "inasmuch as this whole project was based on the recent survey by *Medical Tribune* . . . I called the *Medical Tribune* by long-distance telephone today, and talked with the official in

charge, Mr. Harley Knauer, the advertising manager."
Knauer told Lewis that "four years ago, in the Nixon-
Kennedy presidential fight, *Medical Tribune* took another poll on the identical basis of this one, and it turned
out just the way it turned out this time. The M.D.'s as a
whole, two to one for Nixon, the psychiatrists ten to one
against him."[34]

SEPTEMBER 1

Fifteen hundred delegates to the annual convention
of the New York State American Federation of
Labor and Congress of Industrial Organizations
endorsed the Democrats' national ticket after hearing their president, Raymond R. Corbett, call upon
organized labor to "bury" Senator Barry Goldwater in the Presidential election. The resolution
. . . characterized Mr. Goldwater as one "who would
go it alone along a reckless path at the end of which
lies the devastation of atomic war." Mr. Corbett, in
his address, charged that "Goldwater is trying to
repeal the 20th Century, but we are trying to live
in it." He asserted that "neo-Fascists" and "union
busters" had taken over the Republican Party. "We
will not let them take away our rights and freedom," he said. (*New York Times*, p. 1.)

This gutter rabble-rousing pointedly ignored Goldwater's speech at the Republican parley in Hershey, Pa.,
when he stated: "a Goldwater-Miller administration will
mean an immediate return to the proven policy of peace
through strength which was the hallmark of the Eisenhower years. The Eisenhower-Dulles approach to for-

eign affairs is our approach. It served well the cause of freedom and avoided war during the last Republican Administration. It will do so again."[35]

SEPTEMBER 2

[Goldwater] does not appear to remember with either lucidity or compassion the persecutions, ancient or recent, of the Jews. . . . The Cow Palace at times rang with echoes from the Munich Beer Hall. . . . The danger is that Goldwater may be the precursor of an American totalitarianism. (William Stringfellow, *Christian Century*, pp. 1079, 1082, 1083.)

A week and a half before, Senator Goldwater had made this statement on the floor of the Senate: "I express my support for Senator Ribicoff's amendment to the pending bill. This amendment emphatically reflects the horror felt by the Congress of the United States for the savage persecution to which the Soviet Union is subjecting its Jewish minority. I am sure that civilized people everywhere share the horror we feel and join in the condemnation we express."[36]

SEPTEMBER 6

Senator Goldwater will do his best to excite Americans over the immediate need to combat world communism with a toughness that has so far been avoided. . . . In 1964 the issue will verge on the need for preventive war. (Andrew Hacker, Associate Professor of Government, Cornell University, *New York Times Magazine*, p. 44.)

Three weeks before, in one of his first speeches as Republican candidate for President, Goldwater promised that he would never initiate an attack on a Communist nation, with either nuclear or conventional weapons.[37]

SEPTEMBER 7

Roy Wilkins . . . said in reply to an interviewer's question on what he thought of a possible Goldwater victory: "A Goldwater victory—and God forbid—would bring about what [Goldwater backers] decry in their political campaigning. It would bring about a police state." Pressed for elaboration, the Negro leader restated his view of the effects of a Goldwater victory in these words: "It would lead to a police state. . . ." Mr. Wilkins was interviewed on a taped WNBC-TV program "Searchlight." (*New York Times*, p. 6.)

The indispensable prerequisite of a police state is concentration of power in the executive department of government. It was Goldwater—not Johnson—who was opposing this federal colossus and who championed those individual rights which are always the first to be crushed by a totalitarian government.

SEPTEMBER 7

During NBC-TV's "Monday Night at the Movies," viewers saw this commercial, sponsored by the

Democratic National Committee. . . . A little girl
with wind-tossed hair was shown in a sunny field,
picking daisies. As she plucks the petals of one
daisy, she counts. On the sound track, coming in
stronger and stronger, a male voice counts back-
wards. When the girl reaches 10, the man's voice,
in the doom-filled cadences of the countdown,
reaches zero. The screen is rent with an atomic explosion. "These are the stakes," says the voice of
Lyndon Baines Johnson. "To make a world in
which all of God's children can live, or go into the
dark. We must either love each other, or we must
die." The doom-voice returns, urging viewers to
vote for President Johnson on Nov. 3: "The stakes
are too high for you to stay home." (*New York
Times Magazine*, October 25, 1964, p. 30.)

This same article noted that Democratic Vice-Presidential candidate Hubert Humphrey said he thought the
commercial was "unfortunate". The little girl was part
of a *Time* cover on "The Nuclear Issue". Nearly three
weeks after its first showing, Republican candidate
Barry Goldwater was moved to say, "The homes of
America are horrified and the intelligence of Americans
is insulted by weird television advertising by which this
Administration threatens the end of the world unless all-
wise Lyndon is given the nation for his very own."

SEPTEMBER 9

Senator Fulbright said, "Goldwater Republicanism
is the closest thing in American politics to an equiv-
alent of Russian Stalinism." (*New York Times*, p.
25.)

The high executioners of the feverish left had come full circle. First comparing Goldwater with fascists, they now compared him with Communists.

SEPTEMBER 12

I turned to my other tablemate, who told me that he was an assemblyman from Long Island. When I asked him how he felt about running with Goldwater, he stared moodily into a half-empty highball glass before him and said, "Terrible. I think I'll probably lose. I won't support Goldwater. I won't even vote for him. How can I? I oppose three-fourths of what he stands for. And I'm scared to death of those fanatics. If Goldwater is nominated, this is going to be the filthiest campaign in American history." (*New Yorker*, p. 116.)

Whenever the liberals temporarily ran out of identifiable character assassins, they could always fall back on faceless, nameless tablemates who said they were assemblymen.

SEPTEMBER 12

[In a speech in South Dakota,] after praising the leadership qualities of President Johnson and downgrading those of Senator Barry Goldwater, the Republican nominee, Mr. Humphrey said in one of a half-dozen speeches: "The question before the electorate is simple, prophetic, profound—which of these named do you want to have his hand on the nuclear trigger?" The power of the Presidency is "so staggering," he declared that with "one rash or reckless act 100 million of us would be ashes by nuclear attack." Therefore, Mr. Humphrey continued, "what we are talking about in this election is life itself, the future of the planet, the salvation of the species." (*New York Times*, p. 10.)

A week before, Senator Goldwater had made a statement which, in a calmer age, would have settled the matter for all time. He said, "I do not intend to be a wartime President. I have been to war. I have two fine sons and I do not want them in a war. I have two fine daughters. I have grandchildren. I want none of them touched by war. We seek peace for everyone in this land and in this world."[38]

SEPTEMBER 13

A little girl licking an ice cream cone appeared on millions of television screens all over America. [A woman's voice] . . . told her that people used to explode atomic bombs in the air, and that the radioactive fallout made children die. The voice then told of the treaty preventing all but underground nuclear tests, and how a man who wants to be President of the United States voted against it. "His name is Barry Goldwater," she said, "so if he's elected, they might start testing all over again." A crescendo of Geiger-counter clicks almost drowned out the last words: then came the male announcer's tag-line: "Vote for President Johnson on November third. The stakes are too high for you to stay home." (*New York Times*, September 15, 1964, p. 18).

Republican National Chairman Dean Burch filed a formal complaint with the Fair Campaign Practices Committee about this television spot. Burch said, "This horror-type commercial is designed to arouse basic emotions and has no place in this campaign. I demand you call on the President to halt this smear attack on a United States Senator and the candidate of the Republican Party for the Presidency."[39]

At the request of the Fair Campaign Practices Committee, the Democrats dropped the commercials. The Committee said it had received volumes of mail and phone calls from Democrats and Republicans, all of whom said they were shocked, offended, and angered by what they had seen.[40]

Virtually unnoticed in the furor was scientist Edward Teller's announcement that the United States had developed hydrogen bombs with no radioactive fallout whatsoever.[41]

SEPTEMBER 13

The Rev. Dr. Martin Luther King, Jr. forecast today a "dark night of social disruption" in the United States if Senator Barry Goldwater is elected President. The American Negro leader said he was convinced that the discontent, frustration and despair of disinherited, poverty-stricken groups would then erupt into "violence and riots, the like of which we have never seen before. . . ." There were "dangerous signs of Hitlerism" in the program of the Republican candidate, Dr. King declared. (*New York Times*, p. 66.)

By now it had become a familiar ploy for Martin Luther King to predict violence if his demands were not complied with. He had used this tactic with almost monotonous success in the civil rights struggle; and he had this weapon primed for use in the election. One can only wonder how many votes were swayed by Dr. King's self-serving prophecy of "violence and riots, the like of which we have never seen before", if the country chose to defy him by electing Barry Goldwater.

SEPTEMBER 19

Goldwater is a grotesque burlesque of the conservative he pretends to be. He is a wild man, a stray, an unprincipled and ruthless political jujitsu artist. . . . A crushing defeat for Goldwater will drive the fanatic saboteurs of the Republican Party back into the woodwork whence they came. (*Saturday Evening Post*, p. 80.)

This was the magazine that so sanctimoniously condemned extremism in others.

SEPTEMBER 22

This new Republican party which was born in San Francisco is to be built upon a Goldwater-Thurmond alliance; it is to be a white man's party and not conservative at all, but radically reactionary. . . . Opposition to the Civil Rights Act is by all odds the main reason for his strength in the South. . . . In Barry Goldwater we have a demagogue who dreams of arousing the rich against the poor. (Walter Lippmann, *New York Herald Tribune*, p. 26.)

When it came to Southern segregationists, Lippmann displayed one of the most flexible sets of double standards north of the Mason-Dixon Line. On the one hand, he thundered against Goldwater's association with Strom Thurmond: on the other hand, he never saw fit to comment about Hubert Humphrey's brushing aside questions about Arkansas Governor Faubus' segregationist stands with the remark, "I didn't come down here to get into a squabble with the Governor. . . . I think Governor Faubus has done some very good things in your state."[42]

As for the main reasons for Goldwater's strength in the South, the *New York Times* summarized: "Generally, this Southern Republican strength has three sources. One is the party's traditional stronghold in the Appalachians. The second is among Republicans who moved in from the North and Middle West. The third, and most important, is the growing number of Southerners who see little choice between the racial policies of the two parties, and side with the Republicans for economic and other reasons."[43]

One of the most vicious charges Lippmann hurled against Goldwater was that depicting the Senator as an enemy of the poor, in spite of the Senator's belief expressed in January that "those in trouble through no fault of their own must be helped by society." Goldwater added, "those in trouble through their own fault should always have an opportunity to work themselves out of it."[44]

SEPTEMBER 23

Mr. Meany sharply attacked the record of Senator Barry Goldwater of Arizona, the Republican Presidential candidate, and compared his rise to that of Hitler. Nobody paid much attention to Hitler, Mr. Meany said, but "suddenly the crackpot" took over. (*New York Times*, p. 27.)

The most fervent admirer of Hitler in this country —George Lincoln Rockwell—vehemently opposed Senator Goldwater. During the California primary, Rockwell's American Nazi party circulated anti-Semitic hate literature about Goldwater,[45] and later demonstrated against him in Washington as a "phony conservative" whose family had made large contributions to the NAACP.[46]

SEPTEMBER 24

[In a speech at Terre Haute, Indiana, Humphrey said that] "Mr. Goldwater's freedom is the freedom to be uneducated, to be sick, to be hungry, to be unemployed." (*New York Times*, p. 34.)

Turn to October 17, and note the remarkable similarities between the diatribes of Messrs. Humphrey and Meany. It would be interesting to speculate who was writing whose speeches.

SEPTEMBER 27

Dr. Joachim Prinz, the president of the American Jewish Congress and spiritual leader of Temple

B'nai Abraham warned last night that "a Jewish
vote for Goldwater is a vote for Jewish suicide.
. . ." Dr. Prinz said the Senator was surrounded by
"every hate group in the United States, every anti-
semite in America." (*New York Times,* p. 57.)

Five weeks before, Goldwater had told the Senate,
"We must never forget that the extermination of the
Jews by Hitler was just one manifestation of the inherent barbarism and savagery that are inherent characteristics of the full-blown totalitarian regimes which
seem to flourish in the 20th century like the rankest
of weeds in a poorly tended garden."[47]

SEPTEMBER 27

Hubert Horatio Humphrey, on the high road in
Ohio, Sept. 27: "John Kennedy loved Ohio more
than any other state except his beloved Massachu-
setts. Yet he lost this state in 1960. You owe something to his memory. You have the opportunity to
redeem your state. I want you to undo what you
did in 1960. I want you, in honor of our late President, to go to work between now and Nov. 3. Vote
—and send the message so that John Kennedy in
Heaven will know we won." (*National Review,*
October 20, 1964, p. 895.)

Humphrey did not go so far as to claim Heaven was
voting for Lyndon Johnson—but if his speech had lasted
another minute . . .

SEPTEMBER

The anti-Federalist Goldwater would Balkanize the union, and thus diminish the power with which crusader Goldwater would threaten "the Godless people." (Richard Rovere, *Harper's*, p. 42.) If Goldwater should win . . . there looms, then, the specter of a victorious Republican party, taken over by romantic and conservative activists, and pulled by its own dynamics toward a fascist position. For neither romantic restoration nor conservative preservation is attainable within the limits of the Democratic consensus. If they are to be attained, they must be attained by violence. (Hans J. Morgenthau, *Commentary*, p. 68.)

Here Goldwater was accused of pursuing two diametrically opposed courses of action. Rovere feared Goldwater would make the central government so weak that it would Balkanize the country; but Morgenthau feared Goldwater would make the central government so hyperactive it would be "pulled by its own dynamics toward a fascist position." It never occurred to them that Goldwater—sickened by liberal zig-zags and detours around the Constitution—meant only to restore the separation of powers spelled out by the Founding Fathers "in order to form a more perfect union".

SEPTEMBER

The dangerous economics of Barry Goldwater . . . could rip the fabric of the nation's economic strength, lead to mass unemployment and endanger

America's leadership in the struggle for peace and
freedom. . . . Under the economic philosophy of
Barry Goldwater . . . America would be pushed
back towards the days when employers fired
whomever they wished and dictated wage increases
[sic] or wage cuts, without the check of strong
trade unions or effective collective bargaining.
(*American Federationist*, official monthly magazine
of AFL-CIO, p. 13.)

The unions had delivered prophecies almost as chilling
as the above about the passage of right-to-work laws.
Such laws were passed in many states with Senator
Goldwater's hearty approval—an act that won him the
AFL-CIO's undying enmity, even though the labor
czars could never point to any decrease in union membership in "right-to-work" states. Add to this Goldwater's support for the secret ballot on strike votes and it
was obvious enough why the unions considered the Arizona Senator "dangerous" and spent over $2 million on
"political education" during the election campaign.[48]

OCTOBER 3

[During Goldwater's campaign in the South] some
unsung Alabama Republican impresario had hit
upon an idea of breathtaking simplicity: to show
the country the "lily-white" character of Republicanism in Dixie by planting the bowl with a great
field of white lilies. . . . And springing from the turf
were 700 Alabama girls in long white gowns. . . .
[Goldwater] did not, to be sure make any direct
racist appeals . . . [but] he talked about those reali-

ties all the time, in an underground or Aesopian
language. . . . In the code, "bullies and marauders"
means "Negroes," "criminal defendants" means
"Negroes." "States rights" means "opposition to
civil rights." "Women" means "white women."
(Richard H. Rovere, *New Yorker*, pp. 206, 207,
211.)

It was a grotesque measure of the hysteria of the times
that the color "white" had been placed on the civil rights
groups' subversive list.

In a calmer day, Rovere's scurrilous nonsense about
"Aesopian language" would have been laughed out of
existence. Maddened by Goldwater's refusal to rise to
any racist bait, Rovere sought to attribute to the Senator
indirectly what he could never hope to attribute directly, even if it meant rewriting the dictionary.

OCTOBER 8

Even after this lunatic aberration of American politics has receded and acquired the proportion of a
manageable nuisance, things political in our country cannot possibly return to what they were before. Something must have been quite wrong to
make this aberration possible, and with such a sudden, broad sweep. (Max Ascoli, *The Reporter*, p.
23.)

In reading these venomous outpourings, one almost
wondered if this were 1964 or 1984—with Big Brother
conducting a seek-and-destroy operation against those
remaining conservatives still resisting Heaven-on-Earth!

OCTOBER 14

More than 725 Protestant Episcopal bishops, clergymen and laymen have signed a statement accusing Senator Barry Goldwater and Representative William E. Miller of a "transparent exploitation of racism," it was announced today. The statement charged that the Republican Presidential and Vice-Presidential candidates "are ambitious to be elected by inheriting the votes of white racists, cultivating and harvesting the white backlash." (*New York Times*, p. 20.)

This statement was distributed to the press by William Stringfellow—the same gentleman who had attempted to link Senator Goldwater to the Ku Klux Klan, Adolf Hitler, and totalitarianism in *Christian Century* on September 2. Perhaps the best answer to any racist charge against Senator Goldwater was to be found in this eloquent passage from Theodore H. White's *The Making of the President, 1964:* "The issue of civil rights was as central to American concern in the campaign of 1964 as the issue of war and peace. Yet both candidates jointly decided to exclude from the campaign dialogue as far as possible any implied appeal to racism—and accepting this exclusion with high principle and great responsibility, Goldwater took the loss."[49]

OCTOBER 14

[In a speech in Connecticut, Humphrey] said that "the Goldwater faction" of the Republican party lived "in the conspiratorial police state of their own twisted imaginations." (*New York Times*, p. 20.)

Only a twisted imagination could have strung together that sentence!

OCTOBER 15

Dr. O. J. Hayman, a Maryland Negro who publicly endorsed Senator Barry Goldwater for President, withdrew his support today and threw it to President Johnson.

Dr. Hayman, district superintendent of the African Methodist Episcopal Church said he had reversed his position because of "the excitement generated among the Negro community" and "for the sake of my people."

His original endorsement was made Monday [October 12] at a news conference at the Maryland Republican Headquarters. It brought immediate criticism from the African Episcopal Ministers Alliance of Baltimore and vicinity. (*New York Times*, p. 52.)

It was of course ironic that the champions of "Freedom Now" sought to deny to the political minority within their own ranks the freedom to vote as they pleased.

OCTOBER 16

The chairman of the Federal Maritime Commission was quoted as saying today that election of Senator

Barry Goldwater as President would mean that "the American merchant marine probably would be sunk." John R. Harllee, the chairman, spoke at a meeting of the Texas Breakfast Club today. An information official for the commission, Mike Trupp, quoted Mr. Harllee as saying . . . that if Mr. Goldwater were elected, American shipping "would be wiped off the trade lanes." (*New York Times*, p. 76.)

Within the same week, a telegram from Senator Barry Goldwater was read at a merchant marine luncheon. Goldwater said, in part, "Republicans believe the Federal Government has a legitimate interest in guaranteeing a strong merchant marine as part of our transportation system and our mobilization capability in event of war or national emergency. We are sympathetic about the competitive problem of American shipping faced with lower wage scales and maintenance costs by foreign shipping firms. . . . As President I would initiate a thorough review of our maritime policies toward the goal of finding a long-range solution to insuring a strong merchant marine."[50]

OCTOBER 17

[George Meany said in a fifteen-minute nationwide radio broadcast:] The institution of free collective bargaining . . . has no worse enemy in public life than Sen. Goldwater.
    —To the underprivileged . . . he offers only the freedom to do without.

—To the low-income family, he offers the freedom of the slum.

—To the elderly and infirm, he offers the freedom to seek private charity. . . .

—To the exploited worker, he offers the freedom to work at the lowest wage the worst employer chooses to offer.

—To the jobless worker, he offers the freedom to starve. (*AFL-CIO News*, p. 1.)

This scurrilous denunciation, of course, bore not the remotest resemblance to the Barry Goldwater who had declared in his first speech as Republican nominee a month before: "We, in a Republican administration, shall never abandon the needy and the aged—we shall never forsake the helpless. We understand their problems in our hearts. But we know that a true and lasting solution of those problems cannot be found in degrading, capricious and politically motivated handouts from the White House. It must ultimately be found in a thriving and compassionate economy and in programs principally handled by the levels of government closest to the people."[51]

OCTOBER 17

The purging of the Republican moderates in San Francisco in 1964 was almost as ruthless as Nikolai Lenin's purging of the Mensheviks in 1912. (Stewart Alsop, *Saturday Evening Post*, p. 16.)

Veteran political reporter Richard Wilson of the *Washington Star* wrote that it was "the moderates of the

Republican Party who had drafted the platform. The convention knew this. It knew that platform drafters Melvin Laird of Wisconsin and his associate, Charles Goodell of New York, a Scranton backer, were moderate Republicans seeking enlightened positions on major issues, including civil rights."[52]

OCTOBER 20

Secretary of Agriculture Orville L. Freeman said yesterday that if Senator Barry Goldwater's plan for the abolition of farm subsidies were carried out "25 percent of family farmers would go bankrupt." (*New York Times*, p. 25.)

Three days before, in a speech near Sioux Falls, S.D., Goldwater pledged to his farm audience, "I will never propose a change in the price support system until something better has been developed that can be gradually substituted for it."[53]

OCTOBER 27

[In Madison, Wisconsin,] Senator Hubert H. Humphrey said tonight that the election of Senator Barry Goldwater would make the United States "a garrison state in a nightmare world, isolated from everything except a nuclear reign of terror." . . . Senator Goldwater, Mr. Humphrey summarized, is "dead wrong—tragically, dangerously wrong. The solutions he offers are no solutions at all. They are instead a sure path to widening conflict and ultimately to a terrible holocaust." (*New York Times*, p. 21.)

A week before, Humphrey had summed up what he thought the next three weeks would be like in these words: "the hardest, toughest, and I'm afraid, the meanest of the campaign."[54] He was so right!

OCTOBER 27

In his speech at Jacksonville, Mr. Johnson spoke of the benefits of Federal programs. "Today we are told that Government must abandon many of these programs, and turn them back to the states," he said. "We are told that we must abandon education, we must make Social Security voluntary; we should sell the T.V.A. and get rid of public power, we should forget our farm programs."

Mr. Goldwater has for several months repudiated his previous suggestion that Social Security be made voluntary. Mr. Johnson, however, continued to criticise the Senator on the matter, and at an Orlando shopping center, said: "To strike at the hopes of older Americans is not courage, and when you make Social Security voluntary, you do strike at the Social Security system." (*New York Times*, p. 20.)

It bears repeating that Goldwater had voted for an increase in Social Security payments in 1956, 1958, and 1964.

OCTOBER 31

[In a speech in Idaho, Humphrey said,] "In his hot pursuit of the mirage of total victory, Senator Goldwater wishes to back the Soviet Union into a

corner where its only alternatives would be surrender or nuclear war." (*New York Times,* p.
13.)

On at least three separate occasions in 1964—in an
article written for *Life* magazine in January, a major
foreign policy speech in Santa Barbara, California, in
May, and in his book *Where I Stand,* Senator Goldwater
had spoken not in terms of total victory, but specifically
in terms of *"the reduction of Communist power* to a
level from which it cannot threaten the security of our
nation or the peace of the world."[55] These facts were
readily available to Humphrey, but apparently "the
happy warrior" was never happier than when he was
distorting everything Goldwater stood for.

OCTOBER

President Lyndon B. Johnson in New Orleans: "By
a thumb on a button, you can wipe out 300 million
lives in a matter of moments. And this is no time
and no hour and no day to be rattling your rockets
around or clicking your heels like a storm trooper.
. . . Whose thumb do you want edging up that
way?" (*National Review,* November 3, 1964, p.
944.)

In Akron, Ohio, President Johnson had piously proclaimed, "I don't believe in muckraking or slanderous
comment or mudslinging."[56]

OCTOBER

News item in the *Pittsburgh Press:* "GOLD-
WATER FOE FEARS FASCIST RULE. Election of Senator Barry Goldwater could pave the
way for a fascist take-over of America, Philadel-
phia industrialist Milton J. Shapp fears." (*National
Review*, November 3, 1964, p. 944.)

In October, in his speech at Madison Square Garden,
Senator Goldwater had said, "The Nazi and the Fascist
types—the bigots—they're not going to vote for me because my grandfather was a Polish Jew." Hurrahs broke
out, and he went on: "But do we want these votes?"
"No!" roared the crowd.[57]

NOVEMBER 1

[In a speech at Madison Square Garden,] Mr.
Johnson asserted that the Goldwater forces have
struck repeatedly at "the foundation of our American freedom."
    "Conservative may be written on their banner,"
said the President, "but radical is in their hearts."
The President [said of Goldwater supporters],
"They are not conservatives in the American tradition." . . . [Their] philosophy, the President said,
"is neither conservative nor Republican." (*Los
Angeles Times*, pp. 1, 2.)

Johnson's solicitude for the Republican party and
conservatives couldn't have been more touching—or less
believable.

NOVEMBER 2

In a sermon at the Community Church of New York . . . the Rev. Dr. Donald S. Harrington . . . who is also a vice-chairman of the Liberal Party . . . declared his opposition to Senator Barry Goldwater "because he is an extremist, he supports extremists, he appeals to extremists, and he does not hesitate to divide his country to the core of its very being for the sake of racist votes." (*New York Times*, p. 49.)

To a vice-chairman of the Liberal party, virtually anything conservative was extremist.

NOVEMBER 3

A radio program entitled "Goldwater's New World," in which an impression was given of what might happen if Senator Barry Goldwater of Arizona were elected President of the United States, caused minor panic among listeners in The Netherlands last night. Many listeners called radio stations and newspaper offices to find out what had happened. . . . The program started off with a news bulletin that might be read on Nov. 1, 1967. "Now follows a special bulletin of the radio news services," the announcer said. A newscaster then said: "President Goldwater of the United States has just announced that in view of the continuing state of war, he has just decided that the 1968 Presidential election in his country will have to be postponed." (*New York Times*, p. 23.) If Goldwater wins . . . not only this country but the whole Western soci-

ety would be shaken to its foundations. (Walter
Lippmann, *New York Herald Tribune*, p. 18.)

The Netherlands broadcast was the almost inevitable
climax of months of anti-Goldwater hysteria, fear, and
hate-mongering in this country. By Election Day, the
Goldwater-phobes had frightened the wits out of far too
many Americans—and our allies, as well. Hence this
traumatic reincarnation of Orson Welles' broadcast of
"War of the Worlds"—only this time the Martian was
from Arizona.

NOVEMBER

[Goldwater] is a Doctor Strangelove incarnate, he
is possessed, paranoidal, utterly evil, and close to
suicidal . . . I believe he is close to being an out-and-
out monster. (Maxwell Geismar, literary critic.)
The most important difference, to you and me,
between Adolph Hitler and Barry Goldwater is
that Hitler achieved election in a depression era,
[while] Barry Goldwater has moved onto the
speakers' platform in a time of prosperity, in a
country where militarism has always been scowled
on and rejected, and following hard upon the awesome, monstrous murder in Dallas of one of the
giants of our nation by an "amateur actor" and an
"extremist," too, *so that one can scarcely foresee
history repeating itself*. (Sidney Michaels, play-
wright.) There is undeniably a bit of Goldwaterism in each of us. . . . Now, like a boil, the elements
of American negativism have congregated in one
place. The ugly, tender swelling sits square on our

forehead for all the world to see and taunt. . . . The howl of the brute primeval is the chilling wail that came from San Francisco with the nomination of Barry Goldwater and William Miller. (Louis Lomax, Negro author and lecturer, *Ramparts* magazine, pp. 12, 27, 34.)

This issue was on the newsstands around the middle of October. The front cover featured Goldwater in the body of a rattlesnake.

The liberal Catholic magazine *America* was moved to write of this issue: "This copy represents the Cardinal of Los Angeles as a tyrant. It shows Senator Goldwater both as a snake and as a latter-day Hitler. One may seriously question the conundrums of the Senator's political illogic. But to cast him in the role of modern history's maddest dictator is to practice the most irresponsible extremism. This sort of thing respects neither our national heritage nor our human dignity."[58]

A POST-MORTEM

On November 3, 1964, the voters handed Lyndon Johnson the biggest electoral victory in Presidential history. Johnson defeated Goldwater by 42 million to 26.5 million votes. LBJ's precedent-shattering margin of victory was 15.5 million.

As always—whatever the actual margin of victory—there was much talk of a "mandate" for the winner.

A mandate to do what?

To answer this question, we must attempt to determine what the people understood they were voting for when they voted for Johnson.

The *New York Times* trumpeted that the American people's "overwhelming vote for the Johnson-Humphrey ticket reflects popular attachment to the policies of moderate liberalism."[1] But few voters considered this a head-on clash of liberal and conservative. On the contrary, Johnson's journalistic allies—and even Johnson himself—took great care during the election to blur these terms. Walter Lippmann declared, "There is no more unfounded claim than that Barry Goldwater is a conservative. . . . Senator Goldwater is in fact a radical opponent of conservatism who, under the banner of personal freedom, would compound that moral disorder, which is the paramount problem of the modern age."[2] And as we have already seen, Johnson thundered that Goldwater supporters "are not conservatives in the American tradition. . . . Their philosophy is neither conservative, nor Republican." It was with every justification that F. Clifton White, head of Citizens for Goldwater, commented, "conservatism wasn't defeated in this election; it was hardly even debated."[3]

Conversely, Johnson was almost painfully gun-shy of that loaded word "liberalism". As the Great White Father of Consensus he appeared to live in positive dread of ever being tagged with a label and thereby risking the loss of votes from left or right.

Even the *New York Times*, in a burst of editorial exasperation, complained that "in his frenetic dashing about the country, President Johnson stuck mainly to the safety of pious platitudes, interlarded with cloudy visions of 'The Great Society'."[4] And the Pulitzer Prize-winning reporter for the *Washington Post*, Edward Folliard, frankly acknowledged:

> Unfortunately, perhaps, the 1964 election was *not* a measure of the relative strength of conservatism and liberalism in the United States. President Johnson, seeing the middle of the road wide open, would not call himself a liberal, and would not acknowledge that Sen. Goldwater was a true conservative.[5]

Nor would Johnson acknowledge the issues of the campaign, much to the open distress of the *New York Times*, which groaned:

Rarely in modern times and never in recent years has there been a campaign in which the issues facing the nation have been so inadequately discussed by the two leading candidates; rarely has a campaign added so little to public knowledge; rarely has its end been so welcome.[6]

If the campaign was not a contest of liberal vs. conservative, what caused the great voter stampede to Johnson?

It is the author's conviction that the answer can be found in "A Diary of Defamation". We have seen the unprecedented vituperation leveled against Senator Goldwater, from his victory in the California primary right up until Election Day. The despicable smears—the cries of "fascist", "nuclear madman", "ally of racists", "destroyer of Social Security"—*became* the issues. One did not so much vote *for* Lyndon Johnson as vote *against* the gross caricature of a trigger-happy extremist who, his enemies swore to high Heaven, was going to drop The Bomb and rip up the Social Security cards.

Recall the Fair Campaign Practices Committee's report that a record in the use of political smears might be set in the 1964 election campaign. Writing just a few weeks before Election Day, the FCPC pointed out that the worst of the smears *"are national in scope and effect."* The committee said the election was dull and that consequently vituperation and caricature were playing unaccustomed roles in it. "Usually they distort and obscure content; this time—at least to date—they largely *replace* it," the committee said.[7]

Goldwater realized the urgent importance of bypassing a largely hostile press and reaching the voters directly by means of television programs and commercial spots. But he just didn't have the money for TV in the early months of the campaign; and when the cash finally did come in, there was no time or place left to spend it. As Theodore White told it:

> Since the [Goldwater] headquarters was broke at the beginning of the campaign, Cordiner [the finance chairman] insisted that the precious advance time spots on national television for the last ten days of the campaign—booked in the early weeks with such difficulty from grudging networks—be canceled. When finally in late October, money came pouring into Republican national headquarters like confetti and a desperate effort was made to reinstate these time spots, it was impossible; they had been pre-empted.[8]

At the end of 1964, Goldwater revealed that:

> The bulk of [these campaign contributions] came in in the last two or three days. In fact, it was too late. I wanted to have three more television shows. We didn't have the money. It came in too late. . . . This is hard to believe but we have now almost 1.5 million letters that contained money. Five per cent of the people who voted for us sent money in. I don't think this has ever happened in the history of politics any place in this world.[9]

With only meager advertising on TV, with the newspapers three to one against him* (and publishing all the

---

* In terms of total circulation.

invective that wasn't fit to print), and with some major figures in the Republican party refusing to support him —it was surprising that Goldwater was able to get even 39% of the vote.

There can be little doubt that Senator Goldwater lost votes because of massive confusion about his position on various issues. This confusion persisted partly because of failure to differentiate between Goldwater's stand on a given issue four, five, or six years before, and his stand on that same issue in 1964. *Life* magazine estimated that Goldwater had made at least 3,000 formal speeches since taking his Senate seat in 1953, and that "all in all, Goldwater as a Senator has probably written or spoken on the record *10 million words.*"[10]

To a large segment of the press, it became standard procedure to quote from a Goldwater speech, aside, or ad lib of years past, and ignore his carefully worded position *in 1964* on the UN, states rights, civil rights, Social Security, and arms for peace—all contained in his campaign book *Where I Stand*. At the same time, the newspapers for the most part studiously quoted Johnson's current pronouncements on civil rights and as studiously ignored anti-civil-rights speeches he had made in years past.

Could Goldwater have won in 1964? It seemed impossible, for the same reasons that almost certainly would have precluded victory for any other Republican. Whoever was nominated at the Republican convention in San Francisco would have been running against an incumbent President in a time of prosperity—a President who enjoyed surprisingly strong support from the traditionally Republican business community. At its yearly meeting at Hot Springs, Virginia, a survey of the Business Council found a majority already favoring Johnson. This as early as May! Furthermore, Henry Ford II declared that no matter who the Republican Presidential nominee was, he intended to vote for Johnson.[11] Add to this the almost religious appeal of John F. Kennedy's memory—adroitly captured in Johnson's campaign slogan, "Let us continue"—and the odds became all but insurmountable against *any* Republican Presidential nominee.

Could Goldwater have won a larger percentage of the vote than he did? The author believes he could have, if the liberal Republicans had given him the same unstinting support he had given them year after year in a variety of party roles. But it became apparent early in the game that Goldwater could expect little or no help from this quarter. As early as September, 1963, Arthur Krock had written:

> So long as it appears [Goldwater] may be the Presidential choice of the next Republican convention, the effort to prevent this consummation will be one of the bitterest in American history . . . Some of the most prominent among those who designate themselves as "Eisenhower Republicans" already seem to be prepared to foreclose any victory prospect the party may have in 1964 if they deem this necessary to "stop Goldwater."[12]

They were apparently still prepared to foreclose victory even after Goldwater won the nomination. Three weeks before Election Day, *U. S. News & World Report* confirmed that "in state after state, Barry Goldwater is being forced to carry the burden of the campaign largely by himself."[13]

After Election Day the *New York Times*, which had supported a few Republicans, stormed that "the Goldwater-Miller ticket has dragged down to defeat congressional, state, and local candidates who otherwise would have won."[14] Obviously, the burden of proof was on the *Times* to show which of these candidates "otherwise would have won", but no one bothered to offer the challenge. Certainly it is one of the most venerable political saws that the popularity or unpopularity of a Presidential candidate usually rubs off on his party's state and local candidates. However, the Republican vote in senatorial and congressional races varied widely from state to state. In the South, for example, Goldwater did very well. He helped elect quite a few Republicans in Democratic strongholds. California landed in the Johnson column, but at the same time gave Republican George Murphy an upset senatorial victory over JFK's onetime press secretary, Pierre Salinger. And Californians voted to adopt Proposition 14, a measure that sought to nullify California's anti-discrimination legislation on housing— hardly a reflection of popular attachment to the Johnson brand of "moderate liberalism" so beloved by the *New York Times*.

Nevertheless, there were a few very close races, primarily in the Midwest and Far West. In Ohio, for example, where President Johnson carried the state by over one million votes, Robert Taft, Jr. was only narrowly defeated in his race for the Senate. Taft felt that the "nuclear issue and the Social Security issue definitely hurt Mr. Goldwater very badly, and inevitably had an effect on the other races,"[15] and few would disagree, least of all Senator Goldwater. But the effect could have been minimized for all concerned if more of the Republican candidates had met these issues head-on, even if it meant forming "truth squads" on a state-by-state basis. These "truth squads" could have gone to the *Congressional Record*, and cited chapter and verse from Rep. Craig Hosmer's masterful analysis of the entire nuclear debate. They could have pointed out that in 1960 the late Thomas Murray, a member of the Atomic Energy Commission, publicly underscored the necessity for stockpiling smaller-yield, radiation-free tactical nuclear weapons; and they could have pointed out that in 1964 we still did not have such weapons. On the Social Security issue, they could have quoted from John Chamberlain's column to show that Goldwater was referring to a system of "contracting out", which would allow citizens a choice between public and private old-age pensions.

In setting the record straight—and focussing the spotlight of truth on the vicious accusations against their Presidential candidate—they would have helped not only Senator Goldwater, but themselves as well. But instead, this is what *U. S. News & World Report* found in state after state three weeks before Election Day:

> There are 34 Republican Senators, a number of whom are on the sidelines or seeking to save themselves, and ignoring Barry Goldwater. In the House of Representatives . . . there are 176 Republicans, many of them campaigning for themselves and not for the national ticket.[16]

More than likely, by refusing to refute the fear campaign against Barry Goldwater, Republican candidates lost votes from left *and* right; from liberal Republicans who really believed the GOP had nominated a Dr. Strangelove for President, and from conservative Republicans who resented the candidates' failure to support the Senator. In the end they pleased no one and lost support from both sides.

In New York State, Senator Kenneth Keating asserted that he would have been re-elected if Senator Goldwater had not been the Republican Presidential candidate.[17] It is certainly true that Keating ran far ahead of Goldwater in New York, but he still trailed the victorious Robert Kennedy by over 600,000 votes—a wide voting gap, by any criterion. Keating threw away more than 100,000 votes when he refused to support Senator Goldwater for President. Incensed at his failure to support "Mr. Conservative", the New York State Conservative party put a senatorial candidate of its own on the ballot (Prof. Henry Paolucci) who got nearly 123,000 votes in ultra-liberal New York City alone.[18] There could be little doubt that virtually all of those votes were cast at Keating's expense. But even if the Conservative party had consented to withdraw its senatorial candidate, it seemed highly unlikely that Keating could have defeated the brother of one of the most idolized of Presidents.

It was sometimes excruciatingly difficult to determine just whose side the New York Republican party was on in the Presidential race. Shortly after the Republican convention in San Francisco, the Conservative party asked Republican State Chairman Fred Young to agree on a mutual set of Presidential electors for the Goldwater-Miller ticket. The obvious advantage would have been to secure the votes of Democrats and independents who favored Goldwater but did not want to vote on the Republican line. GOP Chairman Young flatly refused, declaring that the Conservative party leadership had been exposed as a "political blackmail racket". With righteous indignation he added that "the Republican Party in New York never has and never will enter into any political deals with any political group to create a joint set of presidential electors on the ballot."[19] In the absence of any protestations to the contrary, it must be taken for granted that Chairman Young rejected Conservative party support with the consent of both Governor Nelson Rockefeller and Senator Keating.

In October former Vice President Nixon pressed a campaign to "pull the Republican Party together." Nixon went on a speaking tour of 36 states from Maine to Hawaii, winding up on Election eve. He admitted that the GOP's biggest problem was "the Republican defections", which, he said, were running 25% in some states, higher in others. Nixon felt that Republicans had "been in a defensive rather than an offensive posture" in the campaign; he now hoped to put the party "on the attack" across the country. But the former Vice President realized that the difficulty was getting enough Republicans "first to listen, and second to believe".[20] And Nixon was not just talking about the Republican rank and file. At a news conference shortly after Election Day, Nixon surveyed the campaign wreckage and stressed that "Goldwater had the problem of constant sniping from the rear from defectors within his own party." Specifically, he attacked Governor Rockefeller for not having worked for Goldwater in the campaign.

Calling Rockefeller a "party divider", he charged that
the Governor's lack of activity had cost the Republicans
many votes.[21]

Finally, there were no more press conferences. December came and the country got ready to put up a new
calendar. And almost everyone heaved a sigh of relief
that the "vile campaign" was all over.

Or was it?

The emotion-steeped political conflagration of 1964
had run its course. But even today its smoldering embers
remain highly flammable. There can be little doubt that,
in or out of office, Barry Goldwater will be an issue in
congressional and national elections for some time to
come. At the very least, one can expect Democratic candidates to ask their Republican opponents if they voted
for Goldwater for President. And it is predictable that in
some areas Democrats will run against a caricature of
Goldwater just as their predecessors ran against a caricature of Herbert Hoover a generation ago. To refute this
fear campaign against Barry Goldwater has been the
central purpose of this book: to make the little-known,
glossed-over, and buried facts that sustained Goldwater's
position a matter of public knowledge before the cement
of history quite hardens over the hysteria that was 1964.

It is not without irony that two years after the campaign, President Johnson had become almost as disen-
chanted with the Washington press corps as had Senator
Goldwater. In an interview taped for National Educational Television in early 1966, the President's press secretary, Bill Moyers, said that the press in Washington
"tends to write its opinions of a matter, and then to seek
out the facts." Moyers stated that "the President feels

that he is better served, and I share this very strongly, if he can talk directly to the people through radio and television than if the people have to decide upon what some other human being—subject to all the frailties of human nature—interprets as his intentions, or as his policy."[22]

As these closing lines are written, the author wishes to cite one last buried fact, quite possibly the most intriguing one of them all. Predictions had been made that 71 million to 72 million voters would go to the polls in 1964. But the turnout was less than 69 million out of an estimated 113,931,000 Americans eligible to vote.[23] In other words, almost 40% of those eligible to vote in 1964 did *not* go to the polls. Just how much of this stay-at-home vote represents an untapped conservative potential should be the subject of the most intensive inquiry.

It was this "x" factor—the nonvoters of past campaigns—that Goldwater was trying to reach in 1964. The effort must again be made—and again after *that*—in state and national contests.

In any event, it is important to recognize that the bawdy, bloody, blistering 1964 campaign was not a defeat for conservatism per se and did not sound the death knell for conservative influence in this country. Properly understood, it was a beginning, not an end, and conservatives need not apologize for losing a campaign that very nearly equated a Goldwater victory with the end of the world. The important thing is to recognize the absolute necessity for direct communication with the voters through TV and radio, over the heads of the reporters and columnists. And equally important is to underscore what William Rusher, a member of the original Draft-

Goldwater Committee, wrote in the pages of *National Review* after the Republican convention:

> The upsurge of the conservative movement in this country is a development of the first rank. Win or lose in November, we are here to stay.[24]

APPENDIX

Acceptance Speech by Senator Barry Goldwater, Republican National Convention, 1964:

From this moment, united and determined, we will go forward together—dedicated to the ultimate and undeniable greatness of the whole man.

I accept your nomination with a deep sense of humility. I accept the responsibility that goes with it. I seek your continued help and guidance.

Our cause is too great for any man to feel worthy of it.

Our task would be too great for any man, did he not have with him the hearts and hands of this great Republican party.

I promise you that every fibre of my being is consecrated to our cause, that nothing shall be lacking from the struggle that can be brought to it by enthusiasm and devotion—and hard work!

In this world, no person—no party—can guarantee anything. What we *can* do, and what we *shall* do, is to *deserve* victory.

The good Lord raised up this mighty Republic to be a home for the brave and to flourish as the land of the free—*not* to stagnate in the swampland of collectivism —*not* to cringe before the bullying of Communism.

The tide has been running against freedom. Our people have followed false prophets. We must and we *shall* return to proven ways *not* because they are old, but because they are *true*. We must and we shall set the tides running again in the cause of freedom.

This party, with its every action, every word, every breath, and every heartbeat, has but a single resolve:

Freedom!

Freedom—made orderly for this nation by our Constitutional government.

Freedom—under a government limited by the laws of nature and of nature's God.

Freedom—balanced so that order, lacking liberty, will not become the slavery of the prison cell; balanced so that liberty lacking order will not become the license of the mob and the jungle.

We Americans understand freedom. We have earned it, lived for it, and died for it.

This nation and its people *are* freedom's model in a searching world. We *can be* freedom's missionaries in a doubting world. But first we *must renew* freedom's vision in our own hearts and in our own homes.

During four futile years, the Administration which we shall replace has distorted and lost that vision.

It has talked and talked and talked the *words* of freedom. But it has failed and failed and failed in the *works* of freedom.

Failures cement the wall of shame in Berlin. Failures

blot the sands of shame at the Bay of Pigs. Failures mark the slow death of freedom in Laos. Failures infest the jungles of Viet Nam. Failures haunt the houses of our once great alliances, and undermine the greatest bulwark ever erected by free nations—the NATO community.

Failures proclaim lost leadership, obscure purpose, weakening will, and the risk of inciting our sworn enemies to new aggressions and new excesses.

Because of this Administration, we are a world divided —we are a nation becalmed.

We have lost the brisk pace of diversity and the genius of individual creativity. We are plodding at a pace set by centralized planning, red tape, rules without responsibility, and regimentation without recourse.

Rather than useful jobs, our people have been offered bureaucratic make-work. Rather than moral leadership, they have been given bread and circuses, spectacle and even scandal.

There is violence in our streets, corruption in our highest offices, aimlessness among our youth, anxiety among our elders. There is virtual despair among the many who look beyond material success for the inner meaning of their lives.

Where examples of morality should be set, the opposite is seen. Small men, seeking great wealth or power, have too often and too long turned even the highest levels of public service into mere personal opportunity.

Certainly, simple honesty is not too much to demand of men in government. We find it in most. Republicans demand it from everyone—no matter how exalted or protected his position.

The growing menace to personal safety, to life, limb,

and property, in homes, churches, playgrounds, and places of business, particularly in our great cities, is the mounting concern of every thoughtful citizen. Security from domestic violence, no less than from foreign aggression, is the most elementary and fundamental purpose of any government. A government that cannot fulfill this purpose is one that cannot long command the loyalty of its citizens. History demonstrates that nothing prepares the way for tyranny more than the failure of public officials to keep the streets safe from bullies and marauders.

We Republicans see all this as more, *much* more than the result of mere political differences, or mere political mistakes. We see this as the result of a fundamentally and absolutely wrong view of man, his nature, and his destiny.

Those who seek to live your lives for you, to take your liberties in return for relieving you of your responsibilities—those who elevate the state and downgrade the citizen—must see ultimately a world in which earthly power can be substituted for divine will. This nation was founded upon the rejection of that notion and upon the acceptance of God as the author of freedom.

Those who seek absolute power, even though they seek it to do what they regard as good, are simply demanding the right to enforce *their* version of Heaven on earth. They are the very ones who always create the most hellish tyrannies.

Absolute power *does* corrupt. And those who seek it must be suspect and must be opposed.

Their mistaken course stems from false notions of equality.

Equality, rightly understood, as our Founding Fathers understood it, leads to liberty and to the emancipation of creative differences.

Wrongly understood, as it has been so tragically in our time, it leads first to conformity and then to despotism.

It is the cause of Republicanism to resist concentrations of power, *private* or *public*, which enforce such conformity and inflict such despotism.

It is the cause of Republicanism to ensure that power remains in the hands of the people. And, so help us God, that is exactly what a Republican President will do with the help of a Republican Congress.

It is the cause of Republicanism to restore a clear understanding of the tyranny of man over man in the world at large. It is our cause to dispel the foggy thinking which avoids hard decisions in the delusion that a world of conflict will mysteriously resolve itself into a world of harmony—if we just don't rock the boat or irritate the forces of aggression.

It is the cause of Republicanism to remind ourselves and the world that only the strong *can* remain free—that only the strong *can* keep the peace!

Republicans have shouldered this hard responsibility and marched in this cause before. It was Republican leadership under Dwight David Eisenhower that kept the peace and passed along to this Administration the mightiest arsenal for defense the world has ever known.

It was the strength and believable will of the Eisenhower years that kept the peace by using our strength—by using it in the Formosa Straits and in Lebanon, and by showing it *courageously* at all times.

It was during those Republican years that the thrust of Communist imperialism was blunted. It was during those years of Republican leadership that this world moved closer to *peace* than at any other time in the last three decades.

It has been during *Democratic* years that our strength to deter war has stood still and even gone into a planned decline.

It has been during *Democratic* years that we have weakly stumbled into conflict—*timidly* refusing to draw our own lines against aggression—*deceitfully* refusing to tell even our own people of our full participation—and *tragically* letting our finest men die on battlefields unmarked by purpose, pride, or the prospect of victory.

Yesterday it was Korea. Today it is Viet Nam.

We are at war in Viet Nam—yet the President who is the Commander in Chief of our forces refuses to say whether or not the objective is victory. His Secretary of Defense continues to mislead and misinform the American people.

It has been during *Democratic* years that a billion persons were cast into Communist captivity and their fate cynically sealed. Today, we have an Administration which seems eager to deal with Communism in every coin known—from gold to wheat, from consulates to confidences, and even human freedom itself.

The Republican cause demands that we brand Communism as the principal disturber of peace in the world today—indeed, the only significant disturber of the peace. We must make clear that until its goals of conquest are absolutely renounced, and its relations with all nations tempered, Communism and the governments it now controls are enemies of every man on earth who is or wants to be free.

We can keep the peace only if we remain vigilant and strong. Only if we keep our eyes open and keep our guard up can we prevent war.

I do not intend to let peace *or* freedom be torn from our grasp because of lack of strength or lack of will. *That* I promise you.

I believe that we must look beyond the defense of freedom today to its extension tomorrow. I believe that the Communism which boasts it will "bury us," will instead give way to the forces of freedom.

And I can see, in the distant and yet recognizable future, the outlines of a world worthy of our dedication, our every risk, our every effort, our every sacrifice along the way. Yes, a world that will redeem the suffering of those who *will* be liberated from tyranny.

I can see, and I suggest that all thoughtful men must contemplate, the flowering of an Atlantic civilization: the *whole* of Europe reunified and freed, trading openly across its borders, communicating openly across the world.

This is a goal more meaningful than a moon shot—a truly inspiring goal for all free men to set for themselves during the latter half of the twentieth century.

I can see, and all free men must thrill to, the advance of this Atlantic civilization joined by its great ocean highway to the United States. What a destiny can be ours—to stand as a great central pillar linking Europe, the Americas, and the venerable and vital peoples and cultures of the Pacific.

I can see a day when all the Americas, North and

South, will be linked in a mighty system, a system in which the errors and misunderstandings of the past will be submerged, one by one, in a rising tide of prosperity and interdependence. We know that the misunderstandings of centuries are not to be wiped away in a day or an hour. But we pledge that human sympathy—what our neighbors to the south call an attitude that is *simpatico* —no less than enlightened self-interest, will be our guide.

I can see this Atlantic civilization galvanizing and *guiding* emergent nations everywhere.

I know that freedom is not the fruit of every soil. I know that our own freedom was achieved through centuries by the unremitting efforts of brave and wise men. I know that the road to freedom is a long and a challenging road. I know that some men may walk away from it, that some men resist challenge—accepting the false security of governmental paternalism.

I pledge that the America I envision in the years ahead will extend its hand in help, in teaching, and in cultivation, so that all new nations will at least be *encouraged* to go *our* way—so that they will not wander down the dark alleys of tyranny, or the dead-end streets of collectivism.

We do *no* man a service by hiding freedom's light under a bushel of mistaken humility.

I seek an America proud of its past, proud of its ways, proud of its dreams, and determined actively to proclaim them.

But our example to the world must, like charity, begin at home.

In our vision of a good and decent future, free and

peaceful, there must be room for the liberation of the energy and the talent of the individual—otherwise our vision is blind at the outset.

We must assure a society here which, while never abandoning the needy or forsaking the helpless, nurtures incentives and opportunities for the creative and the productive.

We must know the *whole* good as the product of many single contributions.

I cherish a day when our children, once again, will restore as heroes the sort of men and women who—unafraid and undaunted—pursue the truth, strive to cure disease, subdue and make fruitful our natural environment, and produce the inventive engines of production, science, and technology.

This nation, whose creative people have enhanced this entire span of history, should again thrive upon the greatness of all those things which we—as individual citizens—can and should do.

During Republican years this again will be a nation of men and women, of families proud of their roles, jealous of their responsibilities, unlimited in their aspirations—a nation where all who *can*, *will* be self-reliant.

We Republicans see in our Constitutional form of government the great framework which assures the orderly but dynamic fulfillment of the whole man—and we see the whole man as the *great* reason for instituting orderly government in the first place.

We see, in private property and an economy based upon and fostering private property, the one way to make government a durable ally of the whole man, rather than his determined enemy. We see, in the sanctity of private property, the only durable foundation for Constitutional government in a free society.

And beyond that, we see and cherish diversity of ways, diversity of thoughts, of motives and accomplishments. We do not seek to live anyone's life for him—we seek only to secure his rights, guarantee him opportunity to strive, with government performing only those needed and Constitutionally-sanctioned tasks which cannot otherwise be performed.

We seek a government that intends to its inherent responsibilities of maintaining a stable monetary and fiscal climate—encouraging a free and competitive economy, and enforcing law and order.

Thus do we seek inventiveness, diversity, and creative difference within a stable order. For we Republicans define government's role, where needed, at *many* levels, preferably the one *closest* to the people involved.

Our towns and our cities, then our counties and states, then our regional compacts—and *only then* the national government! *That* is the ladder of liberty built by decentralized power. On it, also, we must have balance *between* branches of government at *every* level.

Balance, diversity, creative difference—*these* are the elements of the Republican equation. Republicans agree on these elements and they heartily agree to disagree on many, many of their applications.

This is a party for free men—*not* for blind followers and *not* for conformists.

In 1858, Lincoln said of the Republican party that it was composed of "strange, discordant, and even hostile elements". Yet all of the elements agreed on one paramount objective—to arrest the progress of slavery and place it in the course of ultimate extinction.

Today, as then, but more urgently and more broadly than then, the task of preserving and enlarging freedom at home, and of safeguarding it from the forces of tyranny abroad, is great enough to challenge *all* our resources and to require *all* our strength.

Any who join us in all sincerity, we welcome. Those who do not care for our cause we do not expect to enter our ranks in any case.

And let our Republicanism, so focused and so dedicated, not be made fuzzy and futile by unthinking labels.

Extremism in the defense of liberty is no vice. Moderation in the pursuit of justice is no virtue.

The beauty of the very system we Republicans are pledged to restore and revitalize, the beauty of this federal system of ours, is in its reconciliation of diversity with unity. We must not see malice in honest differences of opinion, no matter how great, so long as they are not inconsistent with the pledges we have given to each other in and through the Constitution.

Our Republican cause is not to level out the world or make its people conform in computer-regimented sameness.

Our Republican cause is not to level out the world or the way for liberty throughout the world.

Ours is a very human cause for very *humane* goals.

This party, its good people, and its unquenchable devotion to freedom will not fulfill the high purpose of the campaign—which we launch *here and now*—until our cause has won the day, inspired the world, and shown the way to a tomorrow worthy of all our yesterdays.

NOTES

HYSTERIA 1964

1. *U.S. News & World Report*, December 21, 1964, p. 47.
2. *Ordeal of the Presidency*, by David Cushman Coyle (Washington, D.C.: Public Affairs Press, 1960), pp. 29, 71, 146, 190.
3. *National Review*, July 28, 1964, p. 641.
4. *New York Times*, October 12, 1964, p. 1.
5. *New York Herald Tribune*, July 17, 1964, quoted in *Congressional Record* (unbound), July 21, 1964, pp. A3804-5.
6. *New York Times*, September 14, 1964, p. 28.
7. *U.S. News & World Report*, December 21, 1964, p. 47.
8. *New York Times*, October 17, 1964, p. 34.
9. *Detroit Free Press*, June 21, 1964, quoted in *Congressional Record* (unbound), June 22, 1964, pp. 14170-1.
10. *Washington Star*, July 8, 1964, quoted in *Congressional Record* (unbound), July 8, 1964, pp. 15570-1.
11. *New York Times*, August 5, 1964, p. 1.
12. *New York Times*, August 8, 1964, p. 2.
13. *Missiles and Rockets*, August 17, 1964, p. 46.
14. *The Making of the President, 1964*, by Theodore H. White, (New York: Atheneum Publishers, 1965), p. 105.
15. *Congressional Record* (unbound), June 10, 1964, p. 12848.

16. *New York Times*, June 3, 1964, p. 42.
17. *Congressional Record* (unbound), June 25, 1964, p. A3484.
18. *New York Times*, August 19, 1964, p. 1.
19. *New York Times*, August 20, 1964, p. 17.
20. *New York Times*, August 21, 1964, p. 8.
21. *New York Times*, September 22, 1964, p. 30.
22. *New York Times*, September 24, 1964, p. 40.
23. *National Review*, October 6, 1964, p. 853.
24. *New York Times*, October 18, 1964, p. 79.
25. *Ibid.*
26. *New York Times*, October 11, 1964, "News of the Week in Review", p. 8E.

EXTREMISM

1. *National Review*, September 8, 1964, p. 756.
2. *U.S. News & World Report*, December 21, 1964, p. 47.
3. *New York Herald Tribune*, July 21, 1964, p. 20.
4. *New York Times*, February 26, 1964, p. 20.
5. *New York Times*, March 9, 1964, p. 18.
6. *New York Times*, March 14, 1964, p. 8.
7. *New York Times*, August 13, 1964, p. 17.
8. *Life*, September 18, 1964, p. 108.
9. *New York Times*, May 24, 1964, p. 48.
10. *New York Times*, July 17, 1964, p. 12.
11. *America*, September 19, 1964, pp. 273-4.
12. *Where I Stand*, Senator Barry Goldwater (New York: McGraw-Hill, 1964), p. 16.
13. *New York Times*, July 19, 1964, Section IV, p. 9.
14. *New York Times*, August 10, 1964, p. 1.
15. *New York Times*, August 13, 1964, p. 17.
16. *New York Times*, January 4, 1964, p. 20.
17. *Look*, October 20, 1964, p. 37.
18. *New York Times Magazine*, August 30, 1964, p. 62.
19. *Look*, October 20, 1964, p. 34.
20. *Ibid.*, p. 37.
21. *Ibid.*, p. 33.

22. *New York Times*, August 25, 1964, p. 1.
23. *Ibid.*, p. 32.
24. *National Review*, September 8, 1964, p. 756.
25. *New York Herald Tribune*, October 18, 1964, p. 26.
26. *New York Times*, October 22, 1964, p. 47.
27. *U.S. News & World Report*, December 21, 1964, p. 47.

THE NUCLEAR ISSUE

1. *National Review*, September 22, 1964, p. 808.
2. White, *op. cit.*, p. 297.
3. *New York Times*, September 13, 1964, Section IV, p. 6.
4. *The Conservative Papers* (New York: Anchor Books, Doubleday & Co., 1964), p. 212.
5. *Life*, January 17, 1964, p. 30C.
6. *U.S. News & World Report*, July 20, 1964, p. 71.
7. *New York Times*, August 26, 1964, p. 29.
8. *New York Times*, August 27, 1964, p. 2.
9. *New York Times*, August 28, 1964, p. 16.
10. *Ibid.*
11. *Ibid.*
12. *Ibid.*
13. *New York Times*, August 27, 1964, p. 2.
14. *New York Times*, September 8, 1964, p. 18.
15. *Ibid.*
16. *New York Times*, September 23, 1964, p. 1.
17. *Ibid.*, p. 33.
18. *New York Times*, October 8, 1964, p. 30.
19. *New York Times*, September 13, 1964, Section IV, p. 6.
20. *New York Times*, September 23, 1964, p. 32.
21. *New York Times*, September 27, 1964, p. 4E.
22. *Ibid.*
23. *Congressional Record* (unbound), September 22, 1964, p. 21770.
24. *Ibid.*, p. 21771.
25. *Ibid.*
26. *Ibid.* Also *New York Times*, September 6, 1960, p. 31.
27. *Ibid.*

28. *The Conservative Papers*, p. 211.
29. *Congressional Record* (unbound), September 15, 1964, p. 21466.
30. *Ibid.*
31. *Congressional Record* (unbound), September 22, 1964, p. 21772.
32. *New York Times*, September 27, 1964, p. 4E.
33. *Time*, September 25, 1964, p. 18.
34. *Ibid.*
35. *New York Times*, September 9, 1964, p. 10.
36. *New York Times*, September 19, 1964, p. 1.
37. *Ibid.*, p. 11.
38. *New York Times*, September 20, 1964, p. 3.
39. *Time*, September 25, 1964, p. 18.
40. *New York Times*, September 20, 1964, p. 3.
41. *Ibid.*
42. *New York Times*, September 22, 1964, p. 3.
43. *New York Times*, September 25, 1964, p. 1.
44. *New York Times*, September 21, 1964, p. 21.
45. *New York Times*, September 23, 1964, p. 46.
46. *New York Times*, September 25, 1964, p. 4.
47. *Washington Star*, September 10, 1964, quoted in *Congressional Record* (unbound), September 15, 1964, pp. A4699-4700.
48. *National Review*, September 22, 1964, p. 808.

THE SOCIAL SECURITY ISSUE

1. *U.S. News & World Report*, October 19, 1964, p. 36.
2. *U.S. News & World Report*, July 24, 1961, p. 52.
3. *New York Times*, May 2, 1961, p. 34.
4. *New York Times Magazine*, November 24, 1963, p. 123.
5. *New York Times*, August 22, 1964, p. 9.
6. *Los Angeles Times*, May 22, 1964, p. 2.
7. *U.S. News & World Report*, December 7, 1964, p. 58.
8. *Where I Stand*, pp. 42-3.
9. *New York Times*, August 22, 1964, pp. 1, 9.
10. *Time*, October 23, 1964, p. 25.

11. White, *op. cit.*, p. 323.
12. *Time*, October 23, 1964, p. 25.
13. *Congressional Record* (unbound), September 30, 1964, p. 22484.
14. *U.S. News & World Report*, December 7, 1964, pp. 58-9.
15. *Ibid.*
16. *Congressional Record* (unbound), September 30, 1964, pp. 58-9.

THE CIVIL RIGHTS ISSUE

1. *New York Post*, September 11, 1964, p. 47.
2. *New York Times*, November 7, 1963, p. 30.
3. *New York Times*, April 17, 1963, p. 22.
4. *Ibid.*
5. *New York Times*, May 9, 1963, p. 17.
6. *Ibid.*
7. *New York Times*, April 17, 1963, p. 40.
8. *New York Times*, May 1, 1963, p. 26.
9. *New York Times*, May 4, 1963, p. 1.
10. *New York Times*, May 8, 1963, pp. 1, 28.
11. *Ibid.*
12. *New York Times*, May 4, 1963, p. 8.
13. *New York Times*, May 5, 1963, Section IV, p. 11.
14. *New York Times*, May 4, 1963, pp. 1, 8.
15. *New York Times*, May 5, 1963, p. 82.
16. *New York Times*, August 30, 1963, p. 1.
17. *Public Papers of the Presidents of the United States: John F. Kennedy 1963* (Washington, D.C.: U.S. Government Printing Office, 1964), pp. 483-4.
18. *Ibid.*, p. 484.
19. *Ibid.*, p. 483.
20. *New York Times*, June 11, 1963, p. 36.
21. *New York Times*, July 2, 1963, p. 28.
22. *New York Times*, August 29, 1963, p. 16.
23. *Ibid.*
24. *New York Times*, August 30, 1963, p. 1.

25. *New York Times*, July 26, 1963, pp. 1, 12.
26. *New York Times*, October 15, 1963, p. 32.
27. *New York Times*, December 16, 1963, p. 17.
28. *New York Times*, April 29, 1964, p. 29.
29. *New York Times*, April 13, 1964, p. 14.
30. *New York Times*, May 30, 1963, p. 16.
31. *New York Times*, October 13, 1964, p. 42.
32. *Congressional Record* (unbound), July 9, 1964, p. 15618. Also see *Congressional Record*, April 10, 1963, pp. 6269, 6271, 6296.
33. *New York Times*, May 24, 1963, p. 1.
34. *New York Times*, July 17, 1963, p. 14.
35. *New York Times*, December 8, 1963, p. 54.
36. *New York Times*, March 16, 1964, p. 25.
37. *Ibid.*
38. *New York Times*, March 13, 1966, p. 45.
39. *New York Times Magazine*, August 18, 1963, p. 16.
40. *New York Times*, April 29, 1964, p. 29.
41. *New York Times*, March 6, 1964, p. 27.
42. *New York Times*, July 1, 1963, p. 16.
43. *New York Times Magazine*, August 18, 1963, p. 86.
44. *New York Times*, September 2, 1963, p. 6.
45. *Ibid.*
46. *New York Times*, July 26, 1963, p. 1.
47. *New York Times*, July 3, 1964, p. 1.
48. *Cornell Law Quarterly*, Winter 1964, pp. 228-256.
49. *Ibid.*, p. 240.
50. *Ibid.*, pp. 252, 254.
51. *New York Times*, May 7, 1964, p. 36.
52. *New York Times*, June 20, 1964, p. 10.
53. *New York Times*, June 11, 1964, p. 23.
54. *New York Times*, June 5, 1964, p. 1.
55. *New York Times*, June 2, 1964, p. 25.
56. *New York Times*, June 9, 1964, pp. 1, 18.
57. *New York Times*, June 11, 1964, p. 24.
58. *New York Times*, June 16, 1964, p. 24.
59. *New York Times*, July 3, 1964, p. 9.

60. *New York Times*, June 19, 1964, p. 18.
61. *Congressional Record*, June 18, 1964, pp. 14318-9.
62. *New York Times*, June 19, 1964, p. 18.
63. *New York Times*, August 7, 1964, p. 1.
64. *New York Times*, July 8, 1964, p. 21.
65. *New York Times*, July 30, 1964, p. 1.
66. *New York Times*, April 17, 1964, p. 18.
67. White, *op. cit.*, p. 236.

THE CALIFORNIA PRIMARY

1. *National Review*, July 14, 1964, p. 570.
2. *U.S. News & World Report*, July 13, 1964, p. 30.
3. *San Francisco Chronicle*, April 16, 1964, p. 1.
4. *San Francisco Chronicle*, April 13, 1964, p. 10.
5. *New York Times*, May 3, 1964, p. 64.
6. *New York Times*, May 14, 1964, p. 26.
7. *San Francisco Chronicle*, April 29, 1964, p. 7.
8. *New York Times*, June 2, 1964, p. 25.
9. *San Francisco Chronicle*, May 7, 1964, p. 14.
10. *Ibid.*
11. *San Francisco Chronicle*, April 27, 1964, p. 1.
12. *Ibid.*
13. *New York Times*, May 17, 1964, p. 72.
14. *San Francisco Chronicle*, April 28, 1964, p. 1.
15. *New York Times*, May 3, 1964, p. 64.
16. *New York Times*, June 1, 1964, p. 13.
17. *San Francisco Chronicle*, April 23, 1964, p. 9.
18. *San Francisco Chronicle*, April 17, 1964, p. 6.
19. *New York Times*, June 6, 1964, p. 9.
20. *Ibid.*
21. *New York Times*, May 27, 1964, p. 21.
22. *Santa Barbara News Press*, May 28, 1964, pp. A-1, A-6.
23. *Los Angeles Times*, May 28, 1964, p. 18.
24. White, *op. cit.*, p. 123.
25. *Ibid.*
26. *New York Times*, May 24, 1964, p. 77.
27. *Ibid.*

28. *New York Times*, June 1, 1964, p. 1.
29. *San Francisco Chronicle*, April 1, 1964, p. 1.
30. *New York Times*, April 20, 1964, p. 20.
31. *New York Times*, October 8, 1964, p. 30.
32. *National Review*, October 20, 1964, p. 912.

A DIARY OF DEFAMATION

1. White, *op. cit.*, p. 201.
2. *New York Times*, July 28, 1960, p. 1.
3. *New York Times*, November 9, 1965, p. 21.
4. *National Review*, October 20, 1964, p. 906.
5. *New York Times*, June 19, 1964, p. 18.
6. *New York Times*, October 21, 1964, p. 31.
7. *U.S. News & World Report*, July 27, 1964, pp. 33-4.
8. *New York Herald Tribune*, July 23, 1964, p. 14.
9. *New York Times*, October 5, 1964, p. 32.
10. *New York Herald Tribune*, September 24, 1964, p. 26.
11. *New York Times*, July 3, 1964, pp. 1, 8.
12. *New York Times*, June 7, 1964, p. 72.
13. *New York Times*, July 18, 1964, p. 6.
14. White, *op. cit.*, p. 198.
15. *New York Times*, July 13, 1964, p. 18.
16. *New York Times*, July 18, 1964, p. 6.
17. *Congressional Record* (unbound), June 25, 1964, p. A3484.
18. *New York Times*, September 27, 1964, p. 1.
19. *New York Times*, October 30, 1964, p. 26.
20. *U.S. News & World Report*, July 27, 1964, p. 77.
21. *Congressional Record* (unbound), September 24, 1964, p. 21992.
22. *Where I Stand*, p. 14.
23. White, *op. cit.*, p. 236.
24. *The Conscience of a Conservative*, by Barry Goldwater, (Shepherdsville, Kentucky: Victor Publishing Co., 1960), pp. 45-6.
25. White, *op. cit.*, p. 200.
26. *Congressional Record* (unbound), August 11, 1964, p. A4223.

27. *New York Times,* October 2, 1964, p. 20.
28. *Congressional Record* (unbound), August 11, 1964, pp. A4226-7.
29. *New York Times,* October 2, 1964, p. 20.
30. *Ibid.*
31. *Congressional Record* (unbound), October 2, 1964, p. A5065.
32. *Fact,* September-October 1964, p. 63.
33. *Ibid.,* p. 29.
34. *Congressional Record* (unbound), August 11, 1964, pp. A4226-7.
35. *New York Times,* August 13, 1964, p. 17.
36. *Congressional Record* (unbound), August 21, 1964, p. 20194.
37. *New York Times,* August 6, 1964, p. 12.
38. *New York Times,* September 4, 1964, p. 12.
39. *New York Times,* September 15, 1964, p. 18.
40. *New York Times,* October 18, 1964, p. 79.
41. *National Review,* October 6, 1964, p. 853.
42. *Time,* September 25, 1964, pp. 21-2.
43. *New York Times,* August 2, 1964, Section IV, p. 9.
44. *Congressional Record* (unbound), August 20, 1964, p. A4422.
45. *New York Times,* May 24, 1964, p. 76.
46. *New York Times,* July 21, 1964, p. 21.
47. *Congressional Record* (unbound), August 21, 1964, p. 20195.
48. *New York Times,* September 21, 1964, p. 36.
49. White, *op. cit.,* p. 304.
50. *New York Times,* October 22, 1964, p. 70.
51. *New York Times,* September 4, 1964, p. 12.
52. *Congressional Record* (unbound), July 20, 1964, p. A3760.
53. *New York Times,* October 17, 1964, p. 16.
54. *U.S. News & World Report,* October 19, 1964, p. 11.
55. *Life,* January 17, 1964, p. 30B. *Santa Barbara News Press,* May 28, 1964, p. A-1. *Where I Stand,* p. 50.
56. *New York Times,* October 22, 1964, p. 45.

57. *New York Times*, October 27, 1964, p. 30.
58. *America*, October 24, 1964, p. 469.

A POST-MORTEM
1. *New York Times*, November 4, 1964, p. 38.
2. *New York Herald Tribune*, October 1, 1964, p. 20.
3. *New York Times*, November 23, 1964, p. 42.
4. *New York Times*, November 1, 1964, p. 10B.
5. *America*, November 14, 1964, p. 587.
6. *New York Times*, November 1, 1964, p. 10B.
7. *New York Times*, October 18, 1964, p. 79.
8. White, *op. cit.*, pp. 318-19.
9. *U.S. News & World Report*, December 21, 1964, p. 49.
10. *Life*, September 18, 1964, p. 94.
11. White, *op. cit.*, p. 255.
12. *New York Times*, September 10, 1963, p. 38.
13. *U.S. News & World Report*, October 19, 1964, p. 35.
14. *New York Times*, November 5, 1964, p. 44.
15. *U.S. News & World Report*, November 16, 1964, p. 66.
16. *U.S. News & World Report*, October 19, 1964, p. 36.
17. *New York Times*, November 25, 1964, p. 22.
18. *New York Times*, November 26, 1964, p. 36.
19. *New York Times*, July 30, 1964, p. 11.
20. *New York Times*, October 2, 1964, p. 22.
21. *New York Times*, November 6, 1964, p. 1, and *U.S. News & World Report*, November 16, 1964, p. 69.
22. *TV Guide*, January 22, 1966, p. A-1.
23. *New York Times*, November 6, 1964, p. 20.
24. *National Review*, July 28, 1964, p. 643.

INDEX